Rejoicing in the Lord Jesus in all Cases and Conditions

together with two sermons:
"The Hope of the Saints in Heaven"
and
"A Christian's Freedom from Condemnation in Christ"

by

Robert Asty
Minister of Jesus Christ in Norwich

"Rejoice in the Lord always, and again I say, rejoice."
Philippians 4:4

Edited by Dr. Don Kistler

Soli Deo Gloria Publications
. . . *for instruction in righteousness* . . .

Soli Deo Gloria Publications
P. O. Box 451, Morgan PA 15064
(412) 221-1901/FAX 221-1902
www.SDGbooks.com

*

Rejoicing in the Lord Jesus in All Cases and Conditions, along
with the two appended sermons, was first published in
London in 1683. This Soli Deo Gloria reprint, in
which spelling, grammar, and formatting changes
have been made, is © 2002 by Soli Deo Gloria.
All rights reserved. Printed in the USA.

*

ISBN 1-57358-139-9

*

Library of Congress Cataloging-in-Publication Data

Asty, Robert.
    Rejoicing in the Lord Jesus in all cases and conditions:
together with two sermons, "The hope of the saints in heaven" and
"A Christian's freedom from condemnation in Christ"/ by Robert
Asty; edited by Don Kistler.
        p. com.
    ISBN 1-57358-139-9
    1. Christian life –Puritan authors. 2. Jesus Christ–Meditations.
    3. Sermons, English. I. Kistler, Don. II. Title.
        BV4509.5 .A84 2002
        248.4'859–dc21

                            2002004053

Contents

Rejoicing in the Lord Jesus in All Cases and Conditions

iii

The Epistle Dedicatory

*To the Congregational Church of Christ in
the City of Norwich*

Dearly Beloved,

It is much to be lamented in any day if many of the righteous are taken away by death (Isaiah 57:1), as being a signal of evil to come, and more so when many eminent ministers of the gospel are so removed, whereby vision fails; and it is most of all to be lamented when the sins of a people and impending judgment threaten their being benighted, and no prospect is given of others to fill up the places of those who are transplanted to eternity.

I know you cannot but have many searchings of heart for your deep share in this matter of lamentation, the Lord having (in so short a measure of time) called home to Himself from among you so many faithful teachers, such as that spiritual man Mr. Armitage, judicious Mr. Allen, and now this laborious Mr. Asty, who served you in the gospel. But it is some matter of refreshment that they, being dead, yet (by their printed labors) still speak to you.

It was the earnest desire of some among you that the ensuing sermons of Mr. Robert Asty might be published. They were taken from his mouth by the pen of a ready writer, and not polished by his own hand; yet they may be exceedingly useful to all for promoting faith, obedience, and comfort.

Indeed, the chief purpose of this treatise is to raise the joy of those who have an interest in Christ, and that in every state and condition. It directs people unto the right object of joy, the Lord, and so to an everlasting ground of rejoicing.

I shall add a few words of counsel to you, for whom I have great respect.

1. Improve the remembrance of those gospel truths which you heard from the mouths of your ministers who are now at rest. Their labors were not intended by the Lord only for a present relief to your souls during their speaking, but for afterward (Revelation 3:3).

Remember how you have received and heard, and hold fast. Beware of losing or growing indifferent as to the practical owning of those gospel principles which you have been grounded in. Be tenacious there; hold them fast, for Christ adds, "If thou shalt not watch, I will come on thee as a thief, and thou shalt not know what hour I will come upon thee."

2. Keep up lively affections towards God when your gospel ministers are withdrawn from you. When David was exiled from the ordinances of God, yet then he had the most earnest pantings of soul after enjoyments of God (Psalm 42:1–2 and 63:1–2: "O God, Thou art my God; early will I seek Thee"). Beware of cooling affections for the institutions of Jesus Christ when you lack them, and let nothing short of God satisfy when you enjoy them. Beware of leaving your first love (Revelation 2:4–5).

3. Maintain frequent spiritual communion with each other when some gospel administrations are lacking. This is prescribed as a means for the prevention of

declinings or departures from God. Hebrews 3:13: "Exhort one another daily while it is called 'today.' " Daily interactions with each other, duly managed, may not only preserve from spiritual decay, but quicken affections, and blow up the spark of your graces into a mighty flame.

4. Wait incessantly in prayer for the return of God's ark to you. The less you have of preaching, the more you should be in praying, and others for you, that gospel light may shine among you as in former days. And the answer will rejoice many and should grieve none; for what hurt can it be to any real Christian that Christ is preached to others?

I shall only add 2 Corinthians 13:11: "Finally, brethren, farewell; be perfect, be of good comfort, be of one mind, live in peace, and the God of love and peace shall be with you."

So prays he who is yours in the Lord Jesus,

Samuel Petto
October 23, 1682

Chapter 1

*The Lord Jesus Christ the Ground of the
Joy and Rejoicing of Believers*

"Yet I will rejoice in the Lord. I will joy in
the God of my salvation." Habakkuk 3:18

Introduction: The Prophet and His Times

Of the stock and parentage of this prophet we have
no clear account in Scripture. This fact may expressly
hint to us that we should always look more to the message than to the messenger, and that nobleness of
birth and greatness among men do not add any dignity
to the Word of God. Indeed, Epiphanius tells us with
some confidence that this prophet was of the tribe of
Simeon, and that he lived in the time of the Babylonian
captivity, but there is little ground for this conjecture.
The time of this prophet's prophesying is also very uncertain. Some Hebrew writers expressly tell us that he
lived in the time of the reign of King Manasseh, and
there is some probability for this assertion. However, it
is clear that he came from the Lord of Hosts; he was
His prophet and he speaks in His name, in much
power and plainness to the people, not fearing the face
of man, and he does not spare to deal closely with that
incorrigible spirit which was among them. The people
had slighted the Lord's message that was delivered by
his predecessors before him, and were now near unto
destruction. Whether it was in the time of the reign of

Manasseh or any other king, modern expositors are very modest in their conjectures and apprehensions, where the issue is not clearly and absolutely determined in Scripture; but this much is certain: it was at that time when God was about to raise up that bitter, cruel, fierce enemy, the Chaldeans, to come out against this people (as you may see in Habakkuk 1:6). At this point God had borne so long with their provocations that the time of His patience had almost expired. Their sins were so multiplied and increased that they were near unto ruin; destruction and desolation were at the door.

Now, this prophet—understanding the mind of God and seeing upon good grounds that the decree was passed against this people, as one who was faithful unto their interest, among whom and unto whom he was the Lord's prophet, and as one who would approve himself faithful unto the Lord—takes upon himself the boldness to expostulate the case with God, why He should suffer such a wicked and vile nation as the Chaldeans to prevail and prosper against His own inheritance, though they were sinful and unworthy. And he cannot rest, neither can he give God any rest, until he hears something further of His mind.

The Lord is pleased to condescend to him in the beginning of the second chapter, and to answer the anxiousness and earnestness of his spirit in this great affair: "And the Lord answered me, and said, 'Write the vision, and make it plain upon tables, that he may run that readeth it. For the vision is yet for an appointed time, but at the end it shall speak, and not lie; though it tarry, wait for it because it will surely come, it will not tarry" (Habakkuk 2:2–3). In short, the Lord makes this answer to him, that though He made use of the Chaldeans as a rod in His hand to scourge His own people with, yet when He had done His work upon His Israel He would take His rod and throw it into the fire, and would deal with all the enemies of His people according to what they deserved. Desolation might come for a while upon the Lord's people, yet they would be raised out of their ruins; but utter desolation and destruction would come upon the enemies of His people. They would at length be brought down and allowed to rise no more. In the third chapter the prophet, according to his name, which signifies "wrestler," wrestles with God, and is another Jacob who will not let the Lord alone until He blesses him.

The Prophet's Prayer and Faith

Habakkuk encompasses God and, in his prayer of wrestling with Him, is very urgent. In this third chapter, he gathers the great experiences that Israel had of God when He walked with them and led them by a strong hand in the wilderness, and he urges those old experiences upon God at this time—how He had dried up the mighty waters and rode in chariots of salvation through the sea for them, and how He caused the sun and the moon to stand still until the enemies of the Lord were cut off and consumed. And he pleads with God based on those experiences, waiting for the same power and the same wonderful appearances and acts for their deliverance out of the present and succeeding troubles that had or should come upon them, just as God had appeared for them and delivered them out of all their troubles of old. And though he tells us that at the first sounding of the words of God's displeasure he was "filled with shakings, and with trembling, and with quivering," yet within a little time he recovered his spirit, and in the exercise of faith in God he glories, rejoices, and triumphs in God alone in the midst of most sinking, most discouraging providences. "When I heard," says he, "my belly trembled; my lips quivered at the voice; rottenness entered into my bones" (verse 16). But see what he says in verses 17–18: "Although the fig tree shall not blossom . . . yet I will rejoice in the Lord. I will joy in the God of my salvation." He saw shakings coming upon the whole earth that put even the foundations, as it were, out of course; he saw God's broom in His hands ready to sweep away all their comforts. An east wind was rising that would blow upon their spring and make all their spring-buds blow off. "Well," says he, "let it be so, or as ill as can be supposed to be, or as ill as a creature can be as to its state in this world, yet I have God on my side, and all is well. I will rejoice in the Lord, I will joy in the God of my salvation."

The Prophet's Joy

This verse is a most noble strain of a heavenly spirit, in the high and constraining exercise of faith in God in a most dismal day of darkness. The prophet gets upon the ruins of the worldly things, and rejoices wholly in Christ; he gets upon the ashes of his house that was burned here, and sings of his building that cannot be burned in heaven; he gets into his withered vineyard and into his barren fields, and there sings: "The lines are fallen unto me in pleasant places. I have a goodly heritage" (Psalm 16:6). It seems a very strange speech, that he should, in the former part of his prophecy, be speaking of the sad dispensations of the Lord towards them, and then in 3:17 speak of great failures that were likely to come upon them, in reference to all their earthly comforts and enjoyments, and yet speak of rejoicing and joying in the Lord! It is a strange thing to talk of joy and rejoicing when he had hardly anything in this world left to him, or supposed to be left to him. "Yet I will rejoice in the Lord. I will joy in the God of my salvation."

We say of some men that it is strange how they live. Their trades fail, their estates are gone, and yet they bear up. Why, it is a mystery how they live, how they have wherewithal to defray their charges. Surely they have some secret friends who feed and maintain them and whom their neighbors do not know of. After the same manner we may speak concerning the Lord's people: they have enemies on every side, they are broken again and again, and yet, behold, they live, and their joy none can take from them, although they are destined to face sorrows and distresses every day! My text tells you the mystery of their living, and of their living in joy, peace, and comfort in the midst of all their losses, troubles, and discouragements: "I will rejoice in the Lord. I will joy in the God of my salvation."

We are "as sorrowful, yet always rejoicing," the apostle says in 2 Corinthians 6:10. This verse unfolds something of the mystery of the verse that we have chosen to be our present text: "As sorrowful, yet always rejoicing; as poor, yet making many rich; as having nothing, and yet possessing all things." So we may say, "Yet I will rejoice in the Lord. I will joy in the God of my salvation."

"I will rejoice in the Lord." The word in the Hebrew is a very full word: "I will rejoice *exceedingly* in the Lord."

Or, "My heart rises like the sea with surges when it is stirred up by the wind." Or, "My heart is like a boiling pot when it seethes." Or (how shall I express it!), "I will rejoice in the Lord. I will magnify myself in God, or make my boast of God in all disasters, and under all discouragements. I will joy in the God of my salvation."

"I will joy": that word also is very full, and it signifies, in its grammatical sense, "My heart shall leap or skip for joy. My heart shall sully forth in my God and take heart in the Lord who never fails." So, "I will rejoice in the Lord. I will joy in the God of my salvation."

One of the ancient fathers, speaking upon this text, said, "Although all the elements should threaten us, and conspire and swear, as it were, a confederacy against us, to turn us out of all things, yet I will rejoice in my God, even in the God of my salvation." And Calvin said, "My joy is not founded upon the creature, nor upon external enjoyments; therefore let all things be brought into confusion here below, nay, let God Himself seem to stand frowning over us, yet, will I rejoice in the Lord. I will joy in the God of my salvation."

The Christian's Joy and the Object of His Joy

Joy is the sweet motion of the soul in a full contentment of heart and complacency of spirit upon some good set before it. Now here the prophet sees all things to be discouraging below, but he turns his eyes up to heaven and sees a certainty and stability there, and therefore he rejoices in the Lord, and joys in the God of his salvation. "I will rejoice in the Lord," that is, "I will rejoice in Jehovah, the God of my salvation." Jehovah is a title given unto God the Father, setting forth His self-existence and self-sufficiency, and His giving being unto all creatures; but the title "Jehovah" is attributed also unto the Son, and so I understand it here in this text: "I will rejoice in Jehovah," that is, in Christ Jesus, who may be called Jehovah not only as He has a sufficiency in Himself, but as He gives existence and being unto all the promises of the covenant of grace, in whom they are "yea and amen." And on this account I take it that the title "Jehovah" is often given unto Jesus Christ, the second Person. "I will rejoice in the Lord. I will joy in the God of my salvation," that is, "in my Lord, my Savior, my dear Jesus, and my Redeemer."

So from the words you may observe this proposition:

DOCTRINE: There is enough in Christ Jesus alone for the soul's full rejoicing and triumphing in all cases and conditions.

"Yet I will rejoice in the Lord. I will joy in the God of my salvation." Let things go how they will in the world, as to my outward concerns, yet the ground of my joy is never taken from me. "Although the fig tree shall not blossom, neither shall fruit be in the vines; the labor of the olive shall fail, and the fields shall yield no meat; the flock shall be cut off from the fold, and there shall be no herd in the stalls," yet my joy abides; the ground of my joy cannot be taken from me. It is not in the creature, it is not upon earth, but it is in heaven; it is not in man, it is in the Lord; it is not in the confluence of these things that are coming and going, and in an uncertain enjoyment, but it is in the Lord who never fails.

David says in 2 Samuel 23:5: "Although my house be not so with God." It is as if to say, "My family is not as I would have it to be. I cannot rectify all the disorders of my house and settle things as I would. My house is not

with God as I would have it according to my heart's desire. Yet God has made with me an everlasting
covenant, and this is all my salvation and all my desire."
The word that is translated "desire" here in the Hebrew
also signifies "delight." So we may read it, "This is all
my salvation, and all my delight. Here is the joy of my
heart; my delight is here. God's covenant of grace
stands sure with me, and therein will I rejoice." It is as if
David had said, "Things go ill with me here below; the
sword is threatened never to depart from my house
while I live, that I must be a man of trouble and of war
to the end of my days. What breaches may be made
upon my kingdom, and what breaches may be made in
my family, the Lord only knows; yet the covenant stands
sure, and that is all my delight. My heart centers here,
and I will comfort myself in the Lord my God."

If we search into the Psalms, there we shall find that
David frequently, amidst great disasters, makes his
boast of God. Providences were frowning, and he
seemed to be driven out of all, yet he says, "The Lord
God is my Refuge. He is the Horn of my salvation, my
Sanctuary and high Tower. I will rejoice, and let all the
righteous rejoice and be glad in Him."

In the handling of this proposition, there are three
particulars that we shall propose to consider and unfold to you, so that the believer may take comfort and
rejoice in Christ at all times, whatever his condition is:

1. What Jesus Christ is;
2. What He has in possession for the benefit and
perfecting of His people;
3. What He will do and is now doing for the believing soul.

PARTICULAR 1. Jesus Christ is glorious in His person, and there is not one like Him in heaven or on earth. What is said concerning Saul in 1 Samuel 9:2 we may in allusion apply to Christ: that he was a choice young man and a good one; there was not among the children of Israel a goodlier person than he. From the shoulders upward he was higher than any of the people. I only allude to it.

Jesus Christ is a most choice, excellent one, a very goodly and a very lovely person. He is higher by both head and shoulders than any of His brethren; a person all glorious, a person all over lovely and beautiful. Song of Solomon 5:16: "His mouth is most sweet; yea, He is altogether lovely, this is my beloved."

But I shall descend into particulars, and show you wherein Jesus Christ is such a sufficient ground of rejoicing and of comfort to the believing soul that has an interest in Him in all conditions. And I shall here show you wherein it appears that the glory of Christ's person is such a ground of rejoicing to us at all times.

That will appear in His mediatorial constitution, as God-man in one person. Jesus is a Mediator (1 Timothy 2:5), an Umpire between God and man to make peace for us (Acts 10:36; Ephesians 2:16–18; Colossians 1:20); and the glory of His person lies in His mediatorial constitution. As He is God-man, so He is a most glorious person (John 1:14). Now this title of "Mediator" is often given to Him in Scripture. In Hebrews 8:6 He is called "the Mediator of a better covenant." In Hebrews 9:15 He is "the Mediator of the new testament." And in Hebrews 12:24 it says, "To Jesus, the Mediator of the new covenant, and to the blood of sprinkling." This was such a one as Job wished for in Job 9:33: "Neither is there any daysman [umpire] betwixt us, that might lay His hand upon us both." Now there are two things that are required for someone to be a mediator. He must be equally related to the persons between whom he comes, and he must be impartial as to each party. Now, both of these qualifications are found in Jesus Christ.

A mediator, I say, must be equally placed between and related to the persons whom he comes to reconcile. A mediator must be a middle person who must not be related more to one person than to the other; there must be an equal proximity or nearness in him unto the parties that he comes to mediate for, or to make peace between. Now, Jesus Christ was such a person in whom there was an equal proximity or nearness to both parties that He had to do with, for He was both God and man. As He was truly man, He stood in a nearness unto man; and as He was truly God, so He stood in a nearness unto the Father. He was by the divine nature as near unto the Father as by the human nature He was near unto man; and He was as near unto man by His human nature as He was unto the Father by His divine nature. So He is equally placed between and related unto the persons whom He came to reconcile.

Also, a mediator must be impartial and faithful in and about the interest of the parties involved. Jesus Christ, being made God-man, was not only in a nearness to man and to the Father, but He was thereby unbiased, and set out upon equal terms impartially to manage the concerns of the interest of both parties. He was both God and man, and was not only so in a nearness to both parties, but He was equally concerned honorably to manage the interest of both parties whom He came between, and was engaged in this nearness that He stood in unto both. He was engaged thereby equally to manage the concerns of both parties. Being God, He was engaged in point of honor to give satisfaction to His Father; being man, He was engaged in point of faithfulness to work out the whole business and concern of our salvation, and to make peace for sinners. He was equally concerned for the interest of both parties, having the divine and the human nature united together in one person. Both natures constrained Him to have an equal and right regard unto both interests, and to bring them into one. It was requisite that Jesus, who was to be a Mediator, should be thus constituted. For, indeed, had He undertaken the work and not been thus constituted, it would probably not have been so impartially managed; neither could Jesus Christ have been complete for the work of His mediation but under this constitution. For if He had been God only, then He would have been too high for the work; for He must make satisfaction. He must suffer and die for sinners. He must be made sin for sinners, and be substituted in the place of sinners. Now, God, absolutely considered, cannot be thus. And if He had been man only, He would have been too low for the work; for there could not have been such dignity in His sufferings as to give a value and worth to all His being laid out for us. He must therefore be God-man, and as such He was neither too high nor too low, but equally placed between both, and so just fitted for the work—and thus do the Scriptures set Him forth to us as Mediator.

The Scriptures Testify of Him as God-Man
  "The Word," that is, the second Person, "was made

flesh" (John 1:14). There is Jesus becoming Emmanuel, God with us (Matthew 1:23). 1 Timothy 3:16: "God was manifest in the flesh." Luke 1:31: "And behold, thou shalt conceive in thy womb, and bring forth a son, and shalt call His name Jesus." Romans 1:3–4: "Concerning His Son Jesus Christ our Lord, which was made of the seed of David, according to the flesh, and declared to be the Son of God with power." So, as you see, He was constituted God-man: "The Word was made flesh." Now, being thus constituted God-man, He had His nearness to God the Father and His nearness to the sons of men, for whom He came and appeared in the flesh. You may see His nearness unto the Father in Zechariah 13:7: " 'Awake, O sword, against my shepherd, and against the man that is My fellow,' saith the Lord of Hosts." So as Jesus Christ He is and He was the fellow and the companion of the Lord of Hosts. Philippians 2:6: "who, being in the form of God, thought it not robbery to be equal with God." Here you see He has His nearness to the Father, and also His nearness to the sons of men, for whom He appeared in the flesh. "Forasmuch then as the children are partakers of flesh and blood, He also Himself likewise took part of the same" (Hebrews 2:14). Isaiah 9:6: "For unto us a child is born, unto us a son is given." Luke 1:35: "The Holy Ghost shall come upon thee, and the power of the Highest shall overshadow thee; therefore also that holy thing which shall be born of thee shall be called the Son of God." He "thought it not robbery to be equal with God." There is His nearness to the Father. And He was born of the virgin, and so clothed with our flesh, and therein He was near akin unto man. Hence He is called "Emmanuel," that is, "God with us."

As God-Man, Christ's Sufferings are Satisfactory

Now, as thus constituted, He undertook the work of His mediation, for thus He suffered and thus He satisfied. His sufferings hereby came to be satisfactory since He was God. He died as man, and He overcame death and arose again from the grave by the power of His Godhead.

QUESTION. But you will say, "This indeed is a great mystery, worthy of all admiration, that the eternal Son of God should become man; that He should be God and man; that there should be a union of the two natures in one Person. But how is this a standing, constant ground of rejoicing in all saddening, sinking providences whatsoever?

ANSWER. I reply, much in every way. And this would be clear to you should I enter upon and open to you the glory of His person as thus constituted, and the glorious excellences of heaven that are shining in both natures, or upon His person under its constitution in the union of both natures. And there may be a greater matter of rejoicing to our souls in the exercise of faith in our contemplating His personal glories. It may be a matter of greater rejoicing to our souls than ever there was satisfaction to the heart and mind upon any object whatsoever that it beheld with a bodily eye. But I shall not go that way, nor enter upon such a prolix discourse, but shall only give you some particulars wherein there is a standing ground of rejoicing for us in Christ Jesus upon His personal constitution as God-man to be a Mediator for us. Here we have dignity, tranquility, sanctity, stability, and communion given to us or brought in upon us.

- Dignity. Hereby is the nature of man raised to

unspeakable honor and glory, in that Jesus Christ, the second Person, has assumed our nature and taken it into union with His own divine nature in His person. And therein He now reigns upon the throne in heaven, at the right hand of God; herein is the nature of man most unspeakably advanced and dignified. The nature of man was very low before. Man was made of the earth, of a little red earth; man was before but a contemptible creature. But now what honor is put upon us, that Jesus Christ has taken our nature and united it to the divine nature; that nature which was despised before is now honored, honorable, and worthy. It has glory and dignity from the Lord Jesus put upon it, says the apostle in 1 Corinthians 15:43–44. The body of man, or the nature of man, both is born and dies in dishonor, aye, but it is raised in glory. The body of man is a corruptible body; it is a dying body. It has a sentence of death hanging over it as soon as it has a being. But now, though it is sown in dishonor, yet it shall be raised in glory. There is a glory that awaits the body of man, that awaits man's whole nature. "Who shall change our vile body, that it may be fashioned like unto His glorious body" (Philippians 3:21). So there is unspeakable honor given unto our nature in that Christ Jesus has taken it so near to Himself, and advanced it upon the Father's throne in heaven.

We are here under the contempt and disgrace of men, but it does not matter, Christians; they cannot take away your glory. The glory of your nature is not laid in the breath of men, but is founded in Christ Jesus' assumption of our nature, and His uniting it to the divine nature. And if, indeed, the enemies of the Lord's people could take our nature from Christ Jesus, then they might take away our glory and our honor; but He has inseparably and everlastingly united our nature unto His divine nature. Therefore our honor is such as can never be taken away.

It is counted a great honor for an ambassador to be sent forth in the name of some great prince to represent him in another country; but, my friends, what is it for Jesus Christ to assume our nature, and to represent man before His Father in heaven? This is a greater honor put upon us than if God had made man the lord of all the angels in heaven. Therefore, let this satisfy you under all the reproach and contempt that you meet with here in the world by one and another. Though you are despised and condemned here and there by a few, yet your honor in the Lord abides.

• Peace and tranquility. In and upon the appearance of Jesus Christ as Mediator for us, there is a full, firm, and lasting peace made between God and us. Jesus Christ came as a Mediator between two parties, to reconcile both and make them one, and this He has done "through the blood of His cross" (Colossians 1:20). Jesus has reconciled God and man together. He has taken away the wrath that the law of God had to pronounce against man. He has slain the enmity of our natures. He has brought these two enemies together and made them one in His own mediatorial hand, so that now you may look unto God, and be at peace with Him. You may see heaven and all the powers of heaven reconciled to you. "Therefore being justified by faith, we have peace with God through our Lord Jesus Christ" (Romans 5:1). And, not only so, but "we also joy in God through our Lord Jesus Christ, by whom we have now received the atonement" (Romans 5:11). Here is the blessing mentioned in the text: "I will rejoice in the Lord. I will joy in the God of my salvation."

But how must I consider Him? Why, consider this Lord as Mediator, making peace through the blood of His cross. And then, Christians, you may joy in God through our Lord Jesus Christ, because it is by Him that you have received the atonement. Jesus Christ has satisfied and reconciled God to you. He has appeased God. He has brought over the heart of God to the sinner, so that now the sinner may take comfort and encouragement in Him, and go to Him as to a Father in Christ Jesus. "But now in Christ Jesus ye who sometimes were far off are made nigh by the blood of Christ. For He is our peace, who hath made both one: (Ephesians 2:13–14). Is not this a matter of rejoicing for you, that now you may go unto God as your God; that you may look up to God and see Him reconciled to you, and see all the properties of His nature looking towards you in a friendly way; that you may see God overruling all providences and dispensations for your interest and advantage; that you may go and comfort yourselves in your God; that you may encourage yourselves in Him, and rejoice in the Lord as your God through the blood of the cross of Jesus your Mediator?

• Sanctification or holiness. Hereby our corrupt natures are sanctified and made holy unto God. Jesus Christ becoming man has consecrated unto the Lord that part of human nature that He came of and belonged to. He has taken our nature and He has offered it up unto the Lord, and so consecrated the whole lump that it was taken out of. This was typified of old by the first-fruits that consecrated the rest; also by the meat offering, of which a part was taken and offered up unto the Lord, and the whole was thereby consecrated (Leviticus 2:1). Now, Jesus Christ comes from that part of the world that was the elect and the chosen of God. He did not come in general from all mankind, though in a general way God has said that all nations are of one blood. Jesus Christ did not come so promiscuously and in general, but He came from that particular part of man that the Lord had chosen and set apart for Himself, and that is the elect of the world. As for reprobates, He did not come from them. He was not of that rank and number, as you may see in John 17:16: "They are not of the world, even as I am not of the world." Verse 19: "For their sakes I sanctify Myself, that they also might be sanctified through the truth." "For their sakes," that is, for those who were the chosen of God, and given to Jesus Christ by the Father. Verse 6: "I have manifested Thy name unto the men which Thou gavest Me out of the world." "For their sakes I sanctify Myself"—He takes our nature and offers it to God, and consecrates it as a part, or the first-fruit of the whole, whereby the whole nature of the elect of God is dedicated to the Lord, sanctified, and made holy, or way is made for the sanctifying of it. I may allude to Romans 11:16: "For if the first-fruit be holy, the lump is also holy; and if the root be holy, so are the branches." I know this is not the meaning of this text; I only allude to it. As the apostle says in that case, so I say in this case: if the first-fruit is holy, the lump is also holy; and if Jesus the Root is holy, then all the branches are holy, to be under a peculiar and special consecration to the Lord.

Now here, Christian, is a ground of rejoicing for you. You are born a child of wrath, your nature is a sinful nature, and there is by nature nothing but sin dwelling in you. But Jesus Christ has taken your nature. He has worn it, and He has consecrated your nature to God, and made way for the sanctifying of it. Therefore now a way is made through Jesus Christ's appearing in our flesh to consecrate you unto God and make you holy, so that you may rejoice, notwithstanding the remains of sin that are in you, and notwithstanding all the impurity and defilements that are to be found in your heart.

You have a stained, polluted soul; you look into yourself, and you see yourself so spotted and defiled that you are ashamed of yourself. Well, then look upon Jesus Christ, and consider how your nature is sanctified in Him. He sits upon the throne all holy, and your nature that He assumed is holy. Why, Christian, there is holiness in the Root for you; there is holiness in Christ your Head for you; and because He is holy, you also shall be holy. Because He has sanctified your nature, therefore your nature shall be sanctified.

"For your sakes," said He, "I sanctify Myself so that you also may be holy. I am holy, and you also shall be holy analogically; that is, in some proportion, in your degree and measure you shall be in a suitableness to My holiness so that you may be made meet for Me." Hence the apostle says, "The very God of peace sanctify you wholly" (1 Thessalonians 5:23); and it shall be so because Jesus Christ has sanctified Himself, and your nature is sanctified in Him. You shall in due time be made holy, and therefore rejoice. Though defiled and sinful for a season, yet you shall be made holy, without spot, and blameless. Christ has made way for this.

• Stability and assurance. Hereby way is made for our

stability, for an eternity and perpetuity for us in grace and in glory. Jesus Christ is a Mediator forever. He has taken our nature to wear it forever. He will never lay aside our nature again, no, not to eternity. Well, therefore, we who are consecrated by Him and reconciled to God by the blood of His cross have a perpetual standing in His grace, and shall have an everlasting abiding in that state of glory unto which we shall be advanced by Him and through Him. All enemies cannot dethrone Christ; ages cannot remove Christ from His throne in heaven, but there He is, and there He shall ever rule and sit. Now, because He sits there, thence is your state in grace sure. If He keeps our nature in conjunction with His own divine nature, then He abides always full and powerful in reference to the concerns that He is to manage, and the work that He is to do for you. He is full of strength, and powerful therein, able to make all effectual. He sits there in heaven to that end. This makes Him so concerned about bringing in and gathering home those for whom He appeared in our flesh. See how Christ concerns Himself for all those for whom He was a Mediator. "Other sheep I have," says He, "which are not of this fold" (John 10:16). In other words, "I have some among the Jews and among the Gentiles. I have some of all nations; these I must gather home." Christ will not lose any; and those who are brought home He will maintain in His grace because He is an ever-living and an everlasting Mediator, and a powerful Mediator.

Under all the temptations, Christians, that you meet with in your way, to cast away your confidence and to renounce your hope in the grace of God, you can still glory and triumph in Christ Jesus, who is our standing

Mediator in heaven. Comfort yourselves in Him, for as long as He abides in our nature He will concern Himself for us; and as He has His eye always upon the glory of God, so also upon the good of sinners. And, being a Mediator, He is carried on with unbiased ends and aims to act impartially and indifferently between both parties. Therefore, while Jesus Christ is Mediator, your state in grace is certain; while Jesus Christ has God's glory to care for, your salvation is sure; for while He concerns Himself for the glory of God, He must also concern Himself with the salvation of His people. These two interests are made one by Jesus Christ the Mediator.

• Familiarity and communion with God. Hereby we have communion with God. Jesus Christ having, as Mediator, made peace for us, now He introduces believers into a comfortable enjoyment of God. Now we may look toward heaven and see God the Father in the face of Jesus Christ. "He therefore that hath seen the Son," said Christ, "hath seen the Father." What! Do you say, "Show us the Father"? What! "Have I been so long time with you, and yet hast thou not known Me?" (John 14:9). In other words, "Do you not know that I have reconciled both together, and made way for communion, that you now, in and through Me, may converse with the Father, as your God and Father?" Jesus, as our Mediator, has given us boldness with God, has let us into the enjoyment of communion with God, and has given us blessed familiarity with God so that now we shall enjoy Him in a gospel way here, and shall have certain hopes of enjoying Him in a glorious way in heaven, ever to be in His presence and to behold His glory. All this comes in by Jesus Christ the Mediator;

and there is no state and condition into which a soul may be brought while he is under grace on this side of heaven but, in that state and condition, he may hold fellowship and communion with God. The three young men did so in the fiery furnace. Daniel did so in the lions' den. Jonah did so in the whale's belly; when he went down into the great deep, yet there he enjoyed communion with God. Therefore, whatsoever your discouragements may be here in the flesh, yet glory in this, that, having peace with God through the blood of Jesus, you may go to Him and say, "Father." You may say, "My Lord and my God." You may converse with Him in the way of the gospel that is consecrated for us to hold and enjoy fellowship with Him in.

Now, Christians, what a ground of rejoicing is here! Friends die; a bosom acquaintance in the flesh is taken from you; they die and their places know them no more. But Jesus ever abides upon the throne, clearing the way of communion between God and you, so that God is always your Friend, always reconciled to you, always ready to make Himself known and to impart His love and grace to you. Here is an abiding ground of joy for us in Christ Jesus, if we consider Him as He is, a glorious person in His mediatorial constitution.

Christ Jesus Is Gracious in His Nature

As Christ is glorious in His person, so He is gracious in His nature. He is full of grace, full of kindness, and full of compassion unto both saints and sinners. He might have appeared glorious in His person and not gracious in His nature. He might have appeared altogether terrible, a glorious person and yet surrounded with terrible majesty; but Jesus Christ is as gracious in

His nature as He is glorious in His person. He is full of
compassion unto the sons of men. There is no harsh-
ness, there is no bitterness in Christ Jesus; there is
nothing in Him, my friends, that will discourage you; if
you search Him ever so closely, there is nothing in Him
to discourage you. He is full of love and full of all encouragement. I do not mean that He is full of love only
as He is God absolutely considered. The apostle says
that "God is love." He speaks it of God the Father; and
so, as Christ Jesus is God equal with the Father in the
divine nature, it is applicable to the second Person. But
that is not all; He is full of grace in His nature as He is
clothed with our flesh. His love is always an encourag-
ing love, it is always a heart-easing love, it is always a
soul-satisfying love. You cannot find such an object
upon earth, nor such an object in heaven, as Jesus
Christ is, that is, so full of compassion and so full of
grace as He is. And the greatness of His love as a
ground of joy unto the believing soul in all conditions
is such as (1) breaks through and conquers all opposition; (2) heightens us under all our sorrows; and (3)
abides unmixed in all seasons.

1. His love is a conquering love. His love is such,
and so great, that it breaks through all opposings and
forbiddings. Though there is nothing in Christ to discourage our love for Him, yet I must tell you that there
is enough in us to discourage Christ's love for us; and,
indeed, there is nothing else in us but that which may
forbid the love of Jesus Christ dealing with us. Now,
whatsoever are the matters of discouragement in us, the
love of Jesus breaks through them all; it sticks at nothing. Let the heart be ever so vile, let the sinner in himself be ever so loathsome, let his ways be ever so con-

trary, let the principles upon which he acts be ever so averse—the love of Jesus Christ breaks through all.

What is the state of a sinner when Jesus Christ comes to visit him? He is in a vile, loathsome, filthy, abominable state. You have it set out in Ezekiel 16 by all manner of strange expressions that show the sinner is in a very loathsome state. Verse 5: You, sinner, laid in your blood and "none eye pitied thee." One cast his eye upon you and said, "There is a loathsome object. I will have nothing to do with him." Another came by and cast his eye and said, "There is a loathsome creature; who would come near such a one?" Again, verse 5: "Thou wast cast out . . . to the loathing of thy person." But, says Jesus, "I passed by you, and it was a time of love." And in Luke 10 you may see it set out in the parable of the Samaritan. One passed by a poor creature who lay in his blood and would have nothing to do with him; another passed by and would have nothing to do with him; but Jesus, the Good Samaritan, passed by and He pitied him, bound up his wounds and healed him.

You may see what forbiddings this love of Christ marches through: "For we ourselves were sometimes foolish, disobedient, deceived, serving divers lusts and pleasures, living in malice and envy, hateful, and hating one another" (Titus 3:3). One would think, "Is it possible that such a soul as this should be brought home and loved by Jesus Christ, who is in such a state, who has such a heart, and who walks in such ways?" But, the apostle says, "The kindness and love of God our Savior toward man appeared, not by works of righteousness which we have done, but according to His mercy He saved us" (verses 4–5). And "such were some of you, but ye are washed" (1 Corinthians 6:11). Jesus loves you notwithstanding this, and continues to love you.

Nay, my friends, this is not all. His love is such as marches not only through great opposings and forbiddings before grace, but high discouragements after grace. Why, what is the walk of the soul after grace? Is it not very crooked and very perverse? Does he not fall short of the rule? Does he not offend God in many things? Is there not a great deal of unbelief? Is there not a great deal of pride, a great deal of carnality, impatience, and passion in your hearts after grace? Do you not stumble and fall in the Christian walk every day, violate the covenant of your state of grace, and break the commandments of God? And yet, notwithstanding all this, He continues to love you (see Psalm 89:30–34). Now, the love of Jesus Christ keeps up through all. "I am persuaded," said the apostle, "that neither death, nor life . . . shall separate us from the love of God which is in Christ Jesus our Lord" (Romans 8:38–39). In the life of a believer after grace, when brought to the test of God's perfect law, there are provocations and unkindnesses between him and the Lord, all his life long, till he comes to the end of his days. And yet, says the apostle, "Life shall not separate."

Now, Christian, this is a great ground of rejoicing, that you may look unto your Jesus and see Him always loving you. Your ways are very uneven and inconstant, and you cannot keep in as good a frame as you would; yet still Jesus loves you. You are full of wanderings, and still Jesus loves you. Why, here is a love that marches through all opposings!

2. His love is a love that heightens us under all our

sorrows (I mean as to the communication and dispensing of it, or the actual and saving discoveries of it unto the believer). It heightens us under all our sorrows, so that the greater our troubles are, the more He loves; and the more pitiful our state is, the more compassionate He is. He sees a believer, it may be, lying under great distresses of body or in great agonies of spirit. This draws out His love; He loves you more, He is the more pitiful and the more compassionate to you, as He sees that your state is a sorrowful state and your condition a troubled condition. And, indeed, the believer never has such discoveries and evidences of the love and kindness of God granted to him as when he is in a low condition. Jesus Christ came, you know, into a wilderness to walk with Israel. And, let their troubles be never so many, Jesus Christ would not leave them. Jesus Christ will not leave you, but, the greater your troubles are, the more is His love revealed, and the more His faithfulness to you will appear.

The people of God never had such eminent and signal appearances of God with them as when they were in their wilderness travels. Jacob, a holy man, never had so much of God, nor such a sight of God, as when he was in a low condition: "Behold, I am with thee, and will keep thee in all places whither thou goest, and will bring thee again into this land; for I will not leave thee until I have done that which I have spoken to thee of" (Genesis 28:15). That good man was in great trouble; he was afraid that he would be cut off, and therefore he said to Laban, "The Lord, the God of Abraham, and the God of Isaac, it was He who rebuked you last night. He charged you that you should speak no hurt, no evil unto me" (see Genesis 31:29, 42). And when Israel came into a groaning captivity and bondage, when their bondage grew very great and unsufferable, then the Lord wonderfully revealed Himself: "And the Lord said, 'I have surely seen the affliction of My people which are in Egypt, and have heard their cry, by reason of their taskmasters . . . and I am come down to deliver them" (Exodus 3:7–8). "The eyes of the Lord are upon the righteous, and His ears are open unto their cry" (Psalm 34:15). Here is a supposition of a condition that the soul is in, or may be brought into, that makes it groan and cry; well, for your comfort, know that then in a special manner the eye of the Lord is upon you, and His ear open to you. Psalm 56:8: "Thou tellest my wanderings." Or, "Thou tellest my flights," so some read it. I never have an enemy pursue me but the Lord takes notice of it, and sees where the enemy hunts me and drives me. He take notice of the fury of the oppressor who comes out against me: "Thou tellest my wanderings, and puttest my tears in Thy bottle."

Every tear in a sorrowful condition Jesus Christ bottles up. He keeps it in remembrance. God's people's highest visits of favor and grace, their choicest experiences, and the most comfortable manifestations that they have of God have come when they have been in a low condition. In prosperity, God many times lets the soul walk more at liberty; and so a believer has less of God in prosperity than in adversity. There he is left to walk by his own light, and he bears himself up more upon his own comforts. He stands then, as it were, more upon his own legs; but in a weak condition, in an afflicted state, in a time of trouble, then is the Lord present, revealing Himself more fully to him. And hence it is that the saints have had their highest joys in the prison, and have been made to sing in the flames. They have described the sharpest distress they were ever brought into as such as could never separate Christ and their souls. The love of Jesus is so great that it will leap into a furnace to keep you company. It is such as will come into any difficulty or danger to support and bear up your spirits. Lo, this is your Friend and your Comforter, O believer, to rejoice in. Jesus' heart is always towards you, and the love of His heart heightens under all your sorrows. Let darkness grow upon your state, the light of His love will shine through it and give you a light so that you can see your way. Let your disconsolations be never so many in the creature, the love of Jesus Christ will countervail all; for if the creature is taken away, Jesus Christ will be all the more. And in the want of all things, He will reveal Himself so as shall answer all to your souls.

3. His love is an abiding love. As His love is such as heightens us under all our sorrows, so it abides unmixed in all seasons. As it is a love that cannot be diverted, so it is a love that cannot be adulterated, but is always a sweet love, a pure love, a heart-easing, soul-pacifying, soul-rejoicing love. None can throw any bitterness into the love of Jesus, but it is always a pure, clear, crystal love that has no mixture in it. It is not thus with the love of friends; there is some mixture in the love of the sweetest, the best, the firmest friends that ever man had upon the earth. They will sometimes rejoice your hearts, and sometimes they will make your hearts sad. Loving friends may sometimes frown and be unkind, and you may go to them with your hopes and expectations and be disappointed; you may soon wear out their love, and they may reveal such a mixture that

their hearts seem sometimes to be alienated. But it is not thus with the Lord Jesus. His love is always a pure, clear, soul-satisfying love; there is light in Him, and no darkness at all; there is sweetness in Him, and there is no bitterness at all. There are, as I said before, things that may encourage you, but there is nothing that will discourage you in Jesus, no, not unto eternity.

Now, believer, this is your Friend. Is not this a Brother born for adversity? Look among all your friends on earth; have you such a one? Look into heaven; are any of the angels able to do for you as Jesus can? Who is there in heaven or earth that your soul can desire in comparison to Jesus? He is glorious in His person, and He is gracious in His nature.

Christ Jesus Is the Exhibitor, Revealer, and Unfolder of a Reconciled God

Jesus is the Exhibitor, Revealer, and Unfolder of all the fullness of the blessed and glorious attributes of God in a way of salvation. God is your God in and through Jesus Christ, and not otherwise. God, absolutely in Himself, dwells in light inaccessible, and is a consuming fire; we cannot make an approach to God, as He is absolutely considered, and live; but now, in and through Jesus Christ, God may be spoken with, and all His attributes, and the properties of His nature, are savingly enjoyable.

There is a great deal of the glory of God that was revealed in the works of creation. There was the glory of His wisdom, the glory of His power, the glory of His goodness, and the glory of His sovereignty. These were revealed in the works of creation; but as so exhibited they are not saving, neither do they afford soul-saving

relief to us, absolutely considered in that primary exhi-
bition that was made of them in the works of creation.
But now, in and through Jesus Christ, all the attributes
of God are saving; all the attributes of God are comfortable and refreshing.

When Adam was outside of Christ, he could not
think of God without it being a terror to him.
Therefore, as soon as he had sinned, fear entered into
his spirit, and he hid himself. "Why!" said he, "I was
afraid, and I hid myself!" Why so? Oh, to consider the
greatness of God and the wisdom of God that were revealed in the creation, the power of God that was revealed in the creation, and the sovereignty and dominion of God that were revealed in the creation; and to
think that he had no interest in this God, that he had
provoked and grieved Him—this was a terror to him. So
Adam said, "Lord, I was afraid, and I hid myself."

Aye, and all the attributes of God are enough to
strike terror into the soul who has no interest in Jesus.
Consider them outside of Jesus, and they are no relief.
But now, in and through Jesus, all God's attributes are
reconciled to and engaged for the believer; and he may
see that which may comfort him and that which may
satisfy him. "But unto them which are called, both Jews
and Greeks, Christ the power of God, and the wisdom
of God" (1 Corinthians 1:24). It is as if Paul had said,
"All the power of God that is saving is in and through
Christ Jesus, and all the wisdom of God that is saving is
in and through Christ Jesus." Therefore in Him, it is
said, are "hid all the treasures of wisdom and knowledge" (Colossians 2:3). Now, if you will but consider the
attributes of God apart, you will find that they are in no
way relieving outside of Christ; but in Christ they are

full of grace, and they are all exhibited and revealed through Him as saving.

• God's justice is satisfied in Christ Jesus. Why, the justice of God outside of Christ is terrible. Consider that God is a most exact, righteous God, who will give everyone their due, and will mete out a portion to everyone according to what he deserves. It is most terrible to consider God outside of Christ, and what may we expect but as Psalm 11:6: "Upon the wicked He shall rain snares, fire and brimstone, and a horrible tempest; this shall be the portion of their cup." This will be the portion of all those whom God has to do with outside of Christ. But now in Christ Jesus this attribute is atoned, and all that wrath, justice, and vengeance had to execute is poured out upon Christ Jesus. Justice dealt with the Lord Jesus in its utmost severity, and received satisfaction in Him and from Him. Now the apostle says in 1 John 1:9, "If we confess our sins, He is faithful and just to forgive us our sins." Romans 3:26: "To declare, I say, at this time His righteousness, that He might be just, and the justifier of him which believeth in Jesus."

Why, justice has nothing to say against you, but it speaks all for you. Because God is a righteous God, therefore He will love you; and therefore He will bless you with all blessings, because He has received full satisfaction from Jesus Christ your Surety.

• God's power is engaged on behalf of believers. Consider the power of God outside of Christ, and it is enough to fill your heart with terror. "Can thine heart endure, or can thine hands be strong, in the days that I shall deal with thee? I the Lord have spoken it" (Ezekiel 22:14). It is as if He had said, "Have you strength to grapple with Me, or can you set your foot against Me?"

No, verily, what are all the nations of the earth? They are less than a crawling worm before the foot of the great God. You cannot stand before it. But now in Christ Jesus this attribute is atoned too, and the mighty power of God is engaged to carry on, and to manage a salvation design in you. Therefore, says the apostle, "That ye may know . . . what is the exceeding greatness of His power to us who believe, according to the working of His mighty power" (Ephesians 1:18–19). So that, let the power of God be ever so great, it is a power engaged for you, to manage and carry on salvation work in you, whatever the opposings are that you meet with, either from your own heart or from others.

• God's wisdom is manifested in Christ Jesus. If you consider the attribute of God's wisdom, it is no relief outside of Christ. That God is so infinitely wise and deep may cause the soul to think, "All this is against me, and what is He now doing but contriving new torments that are more fierce and exquisite for me! And surely there will be no end of these torments!" But now, in Christ Jesus, the wisdom of God is employed in such a design of salvation that the angels are said to pry into it; they are astonished at the design that is brought to light by the wisdom of God.

• God's patience is glorified in Christ Jesus. If you consider the patience of God outside of Christ, it is in no way a relief. For what will it benefit a soul that God bears with it for a while when, under all, there is wrath treasuring up for him against the day of wrath? "What if God, willing to show His wrath, and to make His power known, endured with much long-suffering the vessels of wrath fitted to destruction?" (Romans 9:22). So the patience of God is exercised in bearing with a sinner a little while till he increases his sin; but God will come in upon him, notwithstanding all, though He bears a little while. But now in Christ Jesus the patience of God is reconciled. "The Lord is not slack concerning His promise, as some men count slackness, but is long-suffering to us, not willing that any should perish, but that all should come to repentance" (2 Peter 3:9). Why, God in Christ Jesus is patient; and God glorifies His patience so that He might be known to be gracious.

• God's love is revealed in Christ Jesus. The love and goodness of God outside of Christ are no relief; for they are at an end. The soul may think, "Well, His love is at an end. He has no more love for me. I am His enemy. Man, when he had sinned, had to leave paradise, and God said, "See My face no more." But now, in Christ Jesus, the love, goodness, and mercy of God are revealed.

• The immensity and benignity of God, outside of Christ, are not relieving. God may give you a considerable portion in the world. He may fill your hands with wealth, your house with treasure, and your chest with store. But all this may be given to those with whom God is displeased; there is nothing of love in it, and your fullness is only fitting you for the slaughter. There is the curse of God upon all your store and plenty. This will not at all avail you. But now in Christ Jesus the immensity and benignity of God are reconciled, and how they speak out love and grace! God is an immense God, and He gives out according to His own immensity. And what then are the gifts of His love and grace? They are such as cannot be weighed; they are such as cannot be measured. There is a height, depth, length, and breadth in all His goodness that cannot be fathomed.

And all this He is to the soul through Christ.

• If you consider His eternity outside of Christ, it is in no way relieving. "God is my enemy," says the soul, "and He is an everlasting God. He will be my enemy forever, and all that is in God will be engaged against me forever. His justice, His wisdom, His power, and all His attributes will be engaged against me forever." But now in Christ Jesus the eternity of God is a matter of great comfort to you. Because He is an eternal God, being your God, He will be your God forever, your dwelling place forever, and your portion forever. He will never depart from you. He will never leave you. He will never cease to be what He has promised to be, because He is an everlasting God.

Thus you may run over all the attributes of God; the glory and the fullness of them are exhibited and unfolded, published and revealed, by Christ Jesus unto us. And hence it is in Scripture that the mercy and kindness of God are described to sinners through and with respect to Christ Jesus: "Who hath blessed us with all spiritual blessings in heavenly places in Christ" (Ephesians 1:3). And hence it is said that we, with open face, behold the glory of God in the face of Jesus Christ (2 Corinthians 3:18). "God, who commanded the light to shine out of darkness, hath shined in our hearts, to give the light of the knowledge of the glory of God in the face of Jesus Christ" (2 Corinthians 4:6). And hence it is that Jesus Christ is said to be "the brightness of the Father's glory, and the express image of His Person" (Hebrews 1:3).

So here is another thing that is an abiding ground of joy and rejoicing for us in Christ Jesus. He is the Exhibitor, Revealer, and Unfolder of the fullness of all the blessed and glorious properties of God's nature in a way of salvation. Hence, when God comes to enter into covenant with a believer, He does not enter into covenant with him absolutely, but in and through Christ Jesus. And hence it is that all the promises of the covenant that are God's gifts of grace to us are "yea and amen" in Christ Jesus. Now, do but consider this and you may see that Christ is one in whom your souls may take comfort. Consider the glory of His person as He is Mediator, and consider the graciousness of His nature as He is full of love, and consider how He is the Exhibitor and Unfolder of the fullness of all the blessed and glorious attributes of God in a saving way.

Whatever discouragement, Christian, you have here below, look up to Jesus, and you may see encouragement. Are men engaged against you? Look up to Jesus, and you may see God in Him engaged to be your God. God's power is engaged for you. God's mercy, God's name, and God's glory are all engaged for you. So much for the first particular, what Jesus Christ is.

PARTICULAR 2. We shall now speak to the second particular, and that is what this Jesus has. There are but two things that I shall glance upon under this heading, that may be relieving to us in our looking up to Jesus: He has an irresistible power and He has an inexhaustible treasure.

1. Jesus, in whom we should rejoice at all times, has an irresistible power, a power over every creature in the whole creation of God. "Ye are complete in Him, which is the Head of all principality and power" (Colossians 2:10). Matthew 28:18: "All power is given unto Me in heaven and in earth." Jesus Christ has an absolute do-

minion over all creatures as He is God, and this is a dominion that He received not by gift from the Father, but from the right of creation as He is, with the Father, "over all, God blessed forever." But there is a delegated power, as I may so say, a power that is committed to Christ Jesus by special grant from the Father, as He is Mediator over the whole creation of God. "The Father has placed him far above all principality, and power, and might, and dominion, and every name that is named, not only in this world, but also in that which is to come, and hath put all things under His feet, and gave Him to be the Head over all things to the Church" (Ephesians 1:21–22). Look at Philippians 2:9–11, and there you may see that He received this power from God: "Wherefore God also hath highly exalted Him, and given Him a name which is above every name." 1 Corinthians 15:27: "For He hath put all things under His feet." Psalm 8:6: "Thou madest Him to have dominion over the works of Thy hands." Christ has a universal power as Mediator over the whole creation of God. Now that which is for your comfort in this is that this power is employed and improved for overcoming all your enemies and for filling up of all your wants.

First, this great and universal power that Christ has received over all creatures is improved and employed in overcoming and binding all enemies that are against you. Let your enemies be ever so strong, let the powers of men engage against a poor soul; Jesus Christ has a power greater than them all, will bind them at His pleasure, and will take the prey out of the hands of the terrible. Let Satan, the prince of darkness, assault a poor believer, but he shall never be able to take him and carry him captive; for Jesus Christ will secure him because "greater is He that is in you than he that is in the world" (1 John 4:4). He is greater than the prince and god of this world. Now, the great power that Jesus Christ has is a power for you. Jesus Christ is invested with this power, as He is Mediator, that He might overcome all the enemies of your state and vanquish them at His pleasure; so let them for a while tyrannize and vaunt, yet they shall never be able to carry one poor believer to hell, nor out of the dominion and power of God's grace. For all this power that Jesus has, He is entrusted with for your security.

Second, this power is for overruling all your wants in your state. Jesus Christ has a power, and all power, that He might supply you in all your occasions and necessities. It may be that the poor believer is discouraged; he sees but a little meal in the barrel, but a little oil in the cruse; he sees his stock begin to waste; he thinks he spends upon the principal, and it will soon be all done, and how shall he live then? The water in the pitcher is almost out, the cake that is baked is almost eaten, and the soul begins to think that now it must die. Ah! Christian, this Jesus has all power to answer all your wants; let your necessities be ever so many, do but consider who it is that you have to deal with. It is He who has the fullness of the earth in His own possession. "If I were hungry, I would not tell thee; for the world is Mine, and the fullness thereof" (Psalm 50:12). "The heavens are Thine, the earth also is Thine; as for the world and the fulness thereof, Thou hast founded them" (Psalm 89:11). Whose is the world, I pray? In whose hand is it? Is it not in the hand of your Jesus? Does He not have a dominion over all creatures for you? His mediatorial power is for you, to be improved for you and to be employed for you, so that whatever your necessities are they cannot be greater than your Jesus has a supply for and is able to answer.

You know the thousands of Israelites were called to live for forty years in a howling wilderness, where there was no plowing or sowing, and yet, behold, they were always supplied. They did but cry unto the Lord when they seemed to be in want, and the Lord gave them bread and flesh from heaven. He gave them water out of the rocks, and the fullness of the earth is still in His hand. Elijah was in a low condition and did not know what to do, and God commanded the ravens to feed him. God commanded an angel to be his servant. All the creatures are in covenant for your good. "I have made," said the Lord, "a covenant for you with the beasts of the field, and with the fowls of heaven, and with all creatures" (Hosea 2:18). And if God commands the quails to come and feed the people of Israel, they shall do it. And if God commands the ravens to feed the prophet, he shall not want.

Christ says, "Do ye not yet understand, neither re-member the five loaves of the five thousand, and how many baskets ye took up?" (Matthew 16:9). They were in a little trouble, and reasoned among themselves. "Why," said Christ, "have you forgotten how I fed so many thousands with five loaves and two fishes? My arm is not shortened. My power is not lessened; it is an ab-solute power, an uncontrollable dominion that I have." Therefore, fear not, soul; do not weep over your empty bottle; do not weep over your lost estate; do not weep over your past comforts; but look up to the fullness of Jesus. He has enough for your relief. He can command of the fullness of the earth into your condition, and give it to you by whatever hand He pleases.

2. He has an inexhaustible treasure. It has pleased the Father to put His all-fullness of grace into Him, and to make Him Lord of all that grace that is to be dispensed to believers. "It pleased the Father that in Him should all fullness dwell" (Colossians 1:19). All grace comes from Christ. It is placed in Him as the Fountain, and He has the fullness of all grace for your relief, first unto vital influences and, second, unto actual assistance.

(1) He has a fullness of all grace unto vital influences. Therefore the second Adam was made a quickening spirit, as the apostle tells us in 1 Corinthians 15:45. He has received life that He might give it unto others. The Son of God is said to raise those who were dead. He is a living spring of grace who sends vital grace into our hearts. It is He who implants vital principles of faith, love, patience, and new obedience, who makes us new creatures to God, and who causes us to live before Him. This may be a matter of encouragement to those who are yet dead in trespasses and sins, those who are yet void of grace and destitute of spiritual life. Why, sirs, Jesus Christ is a living spring. Jesus Christ is a quickening spirit, and He gives life to those who are dead. He is furnished with life by the Father to give life to dead souls. Let the dead sinner then hope in Jesus, and let him wait upon Jesus. He who has commanded those who have been dead to live can also command your dead soul to live. He still has life-power and life-grace in Him.

(2) He has all grace for actual assistance. He is the true Olive who empties His golden oil into the hearts of believers. Hence Christ said, "Without Me, ye

can do nothing" (John 15:5). "I am the Vine, and ye are the branches," or, "I am the Root, and ye are the branches." Jesus Christ is an influential Root. He is a root full of sap, full of nourishment, and full of moisture that He conveys to believers for their spiritual growth and improvement. By His strength we are able to stand in a day of temptation; by His strength we are able to manage spiritual duties.

Alas, a little duty would be too great for us were it not for the strength of Christ Jesus; and a little of the grace of Christ Jesus will make a soul wonderfully strong, so that He shall be able to do amazing things, to bear and to suffer astonishing amounts. Oh, how patient will a little of the grace of Christ make the soul under great afflictions! And how it will strengthen a poor, weak believer to hold on in the face of all difficulties! He shall be able to keep pace not only with the footmen, but with the horsemen. By the grace of Christ we are sweetly, swiftly, and joyfully carried on in the ways of new obedience. Hence it is that we are oftentimes commended unto the grace of our Lord Jesus Christ in divers epistles. "I commend you," said the apostle, "to the grace of the Lord Jesus," and, "The grace of the Lord Jesus be with you." Indeed, nothing else is needed, because there is enough for our supply at all times; and therefore, when we are poor, weak, empty, and low in ourselves, we should look up to Jesus as always being full. We know not how to go through such a duty, nor how to manage such a condition; we have not the grace for it, and we think we shall sink and fall under discouragements. Why, Christian, if indeed you had no more than what you have in yourself, you might fear this; but keep your eye upon Jesus. He is full, and filled in order to supply you; and He will communicate according to your necessities. We may, therefore, at all times and upon all occasions, wait upon Him.

PARTICULAR 3. What Jesus Christ will do, and is now doing, for the believing soul may be a ground of comfort and joy to him in all his heart-saddening conditions and tribulations in this world.

1. Jesus Christ appears as an Advocate in heaven at the right hand of God for all believers, answering and silencing all accusations and charges brought in against them, whereby they are continued in the justified state in which they were placed when they first came to God.

There are many failings and provocations in a Christian's way and walking with God. The remains of sin that yet abide in him will be rising up and putting forth into the life and acts of a Christian. But Jesus Christ, as his Advocate in heaven, ever stands up before God to see the peace of a Christian's state kept.

Satan, that old accuser of the brethren, is daily observing a Christian's walking and viewing a Christian's steps, to see if he can gather up anything in his life to censure it, and carry it unto God against him. And believe it, friends, he will not better your case as he represents it unto God. He will not lessen your fault, but will increase it, and make it worse than it is. He is called the adversary of believers in 1 Peter 5:8. The word that we translate "adversary" some read as "a court adversary," one who puts in something against you in the court of heaven. But I would rather read the word to mean one who will charge beyond truth, one that will go beyond the bounds of truth in the charges and accusations that he brings in. For the word in the original imports as much, namely, one who acts against all rules of justice in the pleas that he shall put in or the charges that he shall deliver against a Christian's state in the court of heaven. In Revelation 12:10, he is called "the accuser of the brethren," who accused them before God day and night. He is the old accuser and traducer of the saints at the bar of God's justice.

Now, Jesus Christ always stands up at the right hand of God, there to appear as an Advocate on the believer's account, suing out, on the account of His blood, new pardons for their renewed transgressions, or the continuance of justification and of pardons upon their state, so that nothing may be heard in the court of heaven against them. Jesus Christ stands up to see that a Christian's peace with God is not violated, and therefore He removes sin as fast as it appears. He answers the accusation as soon as it is made, and He silences the adversary as soon as he comes. Hence, "Who is he that condemneth? It is Christ that died, yea rather, that is risen again, who is even at the right hand of God, who also maketh intercession for us" (Romans 8:34). If sin appears, He will remove it; and if Satan steps in, He will silence him. He is there upon this account, as an Advocate to answer for you whenever your name is called into question. And therefore the apostle writes: "My little children, these things write I unto you, that ye sin not. And if any man sin, we have an Advocate with the Father, Jesus Christ the righteous" (1 John 2:1).

As soon as an offense is committed, Christ steps up and pleads your case; and He urges the value of His blood that was shed for the remission of sins so that

your peace with God, into which you were brought in
your first coming over to Him, may be maintained.
Now, Christians, do but consider this and you will find
that it is a ground of joy and comfort in your present
state. It may be that your outward peace is broken in
upon; you have enemies who have disturbed you as to
your outward comforts, and as to your outward joy and
settlement; you have those who have destroyed it. It may
be that your intimate friends are against you and now
stand aloof from you. Well, though it is so, yet your
peace with God abides, and Jesus Christ as your
Advocate keeps you in your justified state before God.
Let the devil do his utmost, he shall never make God
turn against a believer, because Jesus Christ is an
Advocate always at His right hand, speaking for him.
Let him tell ever such stories of a Christian's conduct
unto the Lord, yet he shall never turn God against him.
You know that he did his utmost to turn God against
Job; he told the Lord plausible stories of him, that
there was no truth, no sincerity in him, and that he
served Him but for the comforts of his state, and for the
outward advantages that he enjoyed. But Jesus Christ
saw the peace of Job kept. He was his Advocate then so
early, and He maintained Job in the love and favor of
God—and thus will He do for all believers. He will silence all accusations and remove all objections, and He
will continue you in your state of peace with God.

The virtue of Christ's death is a continued virtue; it
is always influential upon the heart of God for a
Christian. The blood of Jesus is said to be a pleading
blood. "And to Jesus, the Mediator of the new covenant,
and to the blood of sprinkling, that speaketh better
things than that of Abel" (Hebrews 12:24). It is a plead-

ing blood, and it says, "Father, remember the merits of the sacrifice of My death. Remember the satisfaction that Thou hast received, and do Thou continue to love, continue to bless, and continue to delight in and to acknowledge these poor ones, though they fail, and though they provoke Thee." The believer, it may be, is so ashamed of himself upon being overcome that he has not one word to say for himself; he can give no reason why a decree of justice should not go out against him. But the blood of Jesus is always speaking and always interceding, whereby we are kept in that justified state of peace with God that in our first coming over to God we are fixed in. And this may satisfy the Christian under all the disquiets, troubles, and turmoils that he meets with in this world.

2. Jesus Christ is a powerful Intercessor in heaven, daily urging the merits of His death and improving the interest that He has with God to complete the work begun in the hearts of believers, whereby they are growing up to perfection. Jesus Christ is not only an Advocate with the Father, silencing and answering all accusations and charges, and so maintaining the believer in his justified state of peace with God, but, as a lively and living Intercessor, He is always urging the merits of His death, and improving the interest that He has with God to complete the good work of His grace that is begun. Jesus Christ has not only a fountain of all grace for your constant supply, but He acts the part of an Intercessor, and improves the merits of His death to manage the work of grace that is begun in our souls. This you have clearly set forth in Hebrews 9:24: "For Christ is not entered into the holy places made with hands, which are the figures of the true, but into

heaven itself, now to appear in the presence of God for us." Jesus Christ has gone into heaven to appear in the presence of God for us, and He is there to appear not only as an Advocate, but as a mighty Intercessor, pleading with God in the strength of the merits of His own death, improving all His interest with the Father for you.

"In the midst of the throne . . . and in the midst of the elders stood a Lamb as it had been slain, having seven horns and seven eyes" (Revelation 5:6). This Lamb is Christ. Now, Christ Jesus is in heaven, advanced upon a throne for you. He is in the midst of the throne near unto His Father; and how does He sit, or how does He appear? Why, He appears as "a Lamb as it had been slain"; that is, Christ bears the marks of His death before His Father upon the throne. He is there to make a fresh commemoration of His sufferings, presenting His death and His sacrifice before His Father. As Jesus Christ, after He was risen, said unto Thomas, "Come, behold My wounds, and see the print of the nails in My hands and in My feet," so Jesus Christ says, as it were, to His Father, "Father, behold these wounds! Behold how I was pierced! Behold how I was wounded for these people!" And, as one says, "So many wounds, so many cries." Every wound has a crying mouth that is daily pleading with God for the believer. Jesus always stands as a Lamb as it had been slain, urging His death, urging His agony, urging the greatness of His sufferings when justice had Him under the lash, when He trod the winepress of His Father's wrath alone; and He is urging the value of His death for ensuring the success of the work of grace begun, for the increasing of strength, to carry your souls on to perfection.

Jesus Christ lives upon the throne, carrying on this work; and for this great end, He considers the Christian's state in all his dangers, in all his weakness, and under all his wants, and He is improving His death for more grace and for an increase of spiritual blessings. He knows your dangers by reason of your temptations in the world, and He is praying for you there, and improving His interest with His Father on that account: "I pray not that Thou shouldest take them out of the world, but that Though shouldest keep them from the evil" (John 17:15). "O Father," He says, "they cannot stand alone against the temptations of the world in their trades and concerns in the world; let Thy grace be sufficient, and let Thy strength be sufficient to secure them in their dangers." He sees that your grace is yet but small, and will hardly stand against a small encounter; and therefore He prays that it may be increased. "I have prayed for thee, that thy faith fail not" (Luke 22:31). It is as if He had said, "I know that your grace will be sorely tried, and will meet with great opposition; but I have prayed that it may not fail." He pleads with the Father for a more plentiful effusion of the Spirit upon the hearts of His people. "And I will pray the Father, and He shall give you another Comforter, that He may abide with you forever, even the Spirit of truth" (John 14:16–17). And when Jesus Christ prays for the Spirit, He prays that He may come in the royalties of His office into your hearts, bringing in the fruits of grace, of peace, of joy, and of spiritual comfort. And thus, and upon that account, He is called not only "the Author," but "the Finisher of our faith" (Hebrews 12:2).

The intercessory work of Christ is not only at your first coming over to God, to give you favor and peace

with God, but it is a continued act over your whole state
till you come to glory. "He is able to save to the utter-
most," or to carry on salvation work till He has com-
pleted it. Why? Because "He ever liveth to make intercession for us" (Hebrews 7:25). Jesus Christ, by His intercession, delivers out of one strait today, and He will
continue in the same work. And if a new strait appears
tomorrow, He will aid through that also; and He will go
on until He has settled your soul in a complete state of
salvation. Jesus Christ daily exhibits, urges, and presents the merits of His death for the carrying on and
managing of the work that He has begun.

And here take notice, by the way, that when we say
Jesus Christ continues to intercede, you must know that
He does not intercede in a way of free grace, as we do at
the throne of grace. He does not intercede in a precar-
ious way, as believers do, but He intercedes in the merit
of His own sufferings. His interceding is an authoritative act. He not only prays the Father for grace and for
acceptance for us, but He urges the Father upon the account of the infinite price of His own sufferings that
He gave Him, and so does, in an authoritative way, challenge and demand the blessings of His purchase, or of
His death, for the believer. He demands of His Father
the grace that He pleads for; and He, in His interceding act, wills it unto the souls of His people. "Father, I
will," says He, "that they also, whom Thou hast given
Me, be with Me where I am" (John 17:24). And God the
Father always hears His Son. He never denies His Son
any petition that He offers to Him. "I know," says He,
"that Thou hearest Me always" (John 11:42). "Ask of Me,
and I shall give thee the heathen for thine inheritance," says the Father (Psalm 2:8). "Ask, and you shall

have." So as Christ's intercession is a prevailing intercession, it is a powerful intercession; it is always a prevailing intercession.

Now, Christian, do but consider what a ground of joy and comfort this is for you in your present low condition. It may be that you have met with many losses in your outward estate; it may be that you have met with many breakings here and emptyings there, so that your outward comforts are, many of them, gone, and you see others to be very uncertain. Well, but here is Jesus Christ. He is interceding with the Father for more grace, for more spiritual blessings, so that, though you are poor in temporal matters, you are growing rich in spiritual things; though you have but a little of the creature, yet you have grace that is thriving in your heart. And Christ will see that it shall always be increasing and growing. Be not disouraged, therefore, though you have but a little grace and but a little strength. Who knows how much grace the prayer of Christ may bring into thy heart, Christian? Who knows how much strength the prayer of Christ may bring in upon your weak condition to clothe you with? Be not therefore discouraged, though you see your bottle empty and your outward store getting low, seeing that Jesus Christ is carrying on the work of grace in your soul and enriching you with the high and sacred blessings of heaven.

Verily, sirs, if any of you had a friend at court who always sat at the right hand of the king, who had his ear, and a grant of all the petitions that he made to him; and if you knew that he would be always moving the king on your behalf, and pleading with him for some new favors, new advantages, and new places of trust and dignity, and the like—how would your hearts rise in the remembrance thereof! How you would promise yourselves great things in a little while!

Well now, believers, behold and remember that Jesus Christ is your Friend in the court of heaven, who always has the ear of God. And, verily, it is not a vain notion. He is always interceding with the Father on your behalf, pleading for some new blessings, for some further discoveries of His love and manifestations of His favor for your further proficiency in grace, so that you may be carried on unto perfection. Jesus Christ is always pleading this with His Father, so that, though you are very low as to your outward condition, yet you may rejoice that your spiritual comforts are always thriving. They are growing comforts, and your strength in grace is always an increasing strength. Christ prays for it, and makes it so by His daily intercession.

3. Jesus Christ perfumes the spiritual offerings of all believers and presents them unto God as grateful and acceptable, and through Him they always remain as a sweet memorial in God's presence, notwithstanding the weakness and imperfection of them as they come from us.

My brethren, the liquor of our spiritual services has a taste of the vessel through which they pass; there is an ill savor in all our duties as they come from us. There is a great deal of sin, a great deal of self, and a great deal of corruption that mingles with them, defiles them, and gives them an ill savor. But Jesus Christ always stands between God and us. He receives our offerings, refines them, purifies them, cleanses them, and perfumes them, and so makes them a sweet odor, and then offers them up unto God. And hence our prayers come to be prevalent; hence they come to be heard, and to have returns of grace made unto them.

It was Jesus Christ who made Noah's sacrifice so sweet and odoriferous. "And Noah builded an altar unto the Lord, and took of every clean beast, and of every clean fowl, and offered burnt offerings on the altar; and the Lord smelled a sweet savor" (Genesis 8:20–21). Christ Jesus was referred to in his sacrifice, and that made it pleasant, sweet, and fragrant before the Lord.

Christ's sacrifice was typified of old by the high priest's bearing away the iniquities of the holy things of God's people (Exodus 28:36–38). "He shall bear their iniquities," that is, he shall bear them away. He shall receive the iniquities of their holy things and shall bear them away, whereby all shall be hallowed: "And it shall be always," says God, "upon his forehead, that they may be accepted before the Lord," or, "that they may be for an acceptableness before the Lord." Why, Jesus Christ is the gospel of this type. He told His church of old that there must be a priest and intercessor for the sins of their holy things. And so He presents our spiritual offerings unto God refined and purified so that no dross, no manner of sin may be found in them when they are presented before God.

In Song of Solomon 3:6, the Church of God is spoken of as coming out of a dry, barren wilderness condition. Now she comes like pillars of smoke, she comes praying, she comes pleading with God; now her prayers are like pillars of smoke—that is, say some, to set forth their darkness, corruption, and weakness. Our prayers, as they come from us, are more smoke than fire; they are more sin than grace; there is a great deal of corruption upon them that defiles and besmears them. They go up like pillars of smoke, but they are perfumed with myrrh and frankincense, and with all the powders of the merchant—that is, Jesus Christ sweetens them. He perfumes them and makes them offerings of a sweet-smelling savor. "Who is this that cometh out of the wilderness like pillars of smoke?" or, as others render it, "like the smoke of incense." The prayers of God's people ascend like the smoke of incense. Jesus Christ perfumes them with His incense, and so they go up through Jesus Christ as the smoke of incense of old went up to heaven. And this perfumes them, as that which is perfumed by frankincense and by myrrh, and the like. It comes all to one reckoning in whichever sense we take it. It sets forth this much to us, that however spotted, however defiled, and however tainted our duties are as they come from us, Jesus Christ makes them sweet, savory, and pleasant unto His Father. He presents them as a sweet memorial unto Him. Hence, "Even them will I bring to My holy mountain, and make them joyful in My house of prayer; their burnt offerings and their sacrifices shall be accepted upon Mine altar" (Isaiah 56:7).

The believer comes and brings his poor petitions, but they are not fit for the great God to read over, to consider, or to look upon. But Jesus Christ examines them, mends the petitions, draws them up fit to be presented to His Father, and delivers them with His own hand—and then they come to be accepted.

"Ye shall be unto Me," said God unto His Church of old, "a kingdom of priests, and a holy nation" (Exodus 19:6). Now this is applied unto the Church in New Testament days by Peter: "Ye also, as lively stones, are built up a spiritual house, a holy priesthood, to offer up spiritual sacrifices, acceptable to God by Jesus Christ. Ye are a chosen generation, a royal priesthood, a holy nation, a peculiar people" (1 Peter 2:5, 9). You are made a holy priesthood to offer up spiritual sacrifices. Ah, but will they be accepted? Yes, through Jesus Christ, they are acceptable to God.

And again in the Book of Revelation it is said, "He hath made us kings and priests unto God and His Father" (Revelation 1:6), that is, to offer up spiritual sacrifices. But this alone will not do. Jesus Christ stands to receive every offering, and it passes through His refining and cleansing hand and His perfuming incense, and so it comes unto God; and then it is a valuable sacrifice. Then it is a pleasant and delightful sacrifice. He puts it into His golden censer and offers it up to His Father (as in Revelation 8:3). Here is the great mystery of the intercession of Jesus Christ held forth to you, in reference to your spiritual oblations. He had a golden censer, "and there was given unto Him much incense." He has enough for all your prayers. There was given Him much incense "that He should offer it with the prayers of all saints." So we read it; but it might also be read, "that He should add it unto the prayers of all saints," importing that our prayers are not weighty as they come from us, nor acceptable, but they have the incense of Christ Jesus added to them, and *then* they are weighty; *then* they are acceptable. And from hence God the Father comes to be delighted in the supplications of His servants.

Now, Christians, by the way, I beseech you, take this notion into your faith. It is generally received and believed that we must rest upon the satisfaction of Christ Jesus for the acceptance of our persons. Let me tell you that you must also act faith upon Jesus Christ as an

Intercessor, and rest upon the merits of His incense and of His mediation for all your success in your approaches unto God. As you must act faith upon the merits of Christ Jesus for the acceptance of your persons, so you must act faith upon the merits of Christ's death, and of Christ's life now in heaven, for the acceptance of all your spiritual performances with God. And here, my brethren, you have another ground of joy and comfort in your low estate here. Suppose that you are tossed to and fro by many tempests; suppose that you are sorely broken by breaches of providence; suppose that you have lost many dear friends that you used to consult with and to go to for assistance. Why, yet you have Jesus Christ keeping your way clear unto the Father, and it is He who gives you a constant boldness with Him. Bring all your petitions; ask what you will in the name of Christ Jesus, and it shall be granted to you. Christ stands ready to receive your petitions, to mend whatsoever is amiss in them, and to present them in His own way unto His Father so that they may be accepted.

In and through Christ you have a liberty and boldness with God. "Let us come boldly," says the apostle, "unto the throne of grace" (Hebrews 4:16). And in Hebrews 10:19 we read: "Having, therefore, brethren, boldness to enter into the holiest by the blood of Jesus." Jesus Christ will not throw out a petition because it was not better worded. Jesus Christ will not throw back a prayer because the spirit was not more composed and ordered in it. Jesus Christ will not throw back a duty because He sees a little unbelief in it, or something of self in it, or something that is displeasing to His Father in it; rather He takes out whatsoever is displeasing, adds His own incense to it, carries it unto His Father, and delivers it as an acceptable offering unto Him. And on this ground you may joy and rejoice in the Lord Jesus, whatever your condition is in this world.

4. Jesus Christ in wisdom directs, and with love and grace influences, all the losses, crosses, and afflictions of your Christian state, whereby they are all made to further your spiritual interest and to be greatly subservient to your soul's advantage. It is the lot and portion of God's people to be often afflicted, to be sorely broken, as in the place of dragons; and they are many times emptied from vessel to vessel. But, Christian, there is infinite wisdom, infinite reconciled wisdom, that orders all the motions of providence in all the changes of your condition. Jesus Christ has hold of every providence. And He directs it in wisdom, and influences it with love and grace, so that it must do you good; it cannot be to your harm or prejudice. "God hath put all things under His feet, and gave Him to be the Head over all things to the Church" (Ephesians 1:22). Christ's providential kingdom is subordinate unto His spiritual kingdom, unto which you belong; and by His grace and wisdom He directs all, and in mercy manages all, for your advantage. "The eyes of the Lord are upon the righteous, and His ears are open unto their cry" (Psalm 34:15).

The Lord Jesus is ever viewing a Christian's state, in his going out, his coming in, his lying down, and his rising up. He is ever viewing a Christian's condition, and in wisdom directs all for the best. It is therefore said, and it is a notable Scripture, "As for their rings, they were so high that they were dreadful; and their

rings were full of eyes, round about them four" (Ezekiel
1:18). The prophet is here speaking of the great mystery
of providence. "Sometimes," he says, "God's providences are very deep; they are very tremendous and
dreadful. But, be it so, the rings of the wheels of providence are always full of eyes; round about them four,
they are full of eyes." That is wisdom directing, guiding,
influencing, and managing. "Now," says he, "the rings
of the wheels that move in every state and condition are
always full of eyes. There is not only an eye one way, but
there is an eye that looks every way. The wheels of providence are full of eyes." There are many eyes. Jesus
Christ observes, and He looks closely, and in His infinite wisdom He directs for the best. There are eyes in
the wheels.

Things do not casually come upon you; things do
not come upon you by chance, but the wheel that is full
of eyes moves, Christians, in all your troubles, in all
your losses, and in all your crosses. And by the eye of
God that is upon your condition, that sets the wheel going, He observes and takes notice of what is best for
you. When it is seasonable to make a breach, then a
breach shall be made; when it is seasonable to take
away a comfort, then a comfort shall be taken away;
when it is seasonable to let a temptation loose, then a
temptation shall come; when it is seasonable to put you
upon a trial, then the trial shall appear. The rings are
full of eyes. There is wisdom that directs the providences of a Christian's state. I pray, mark this Scripture:
"If need be, ye are in heaviness through manifold temptations" (1 Peter 1:6). The eyes of the wheels observe
when it is needful to come in with a change of providence, when it is needful to let Satan loose upon you,

when it is needful to bring a cross into your condition, and when it is needful to bring an affliction upon you, to lay a wound upon your bodies or a weight upon your spirits. "If need be, ye are in heaviness through manifold temptations"; the temptation does not come until you need it. God sees when it is time to bind and when it is time to loosen; when it is time to enlarge and when it is time to constrain; when it is time to give and when it is time to take; and whether it needs to be a certain way with you.

As the Lord oversees all matters of affliction, so also the coming in of comfort. Wherefore, says the apostle, "Let us therefore come boldly unto the throne of grace, that we may obtain mercy, and find grace to help in time of need" (Hebrews 4:16).

When God sees that you need more strength or more grace, you shall have it; when God sees that you need more comfort or more peace, you shall have it; so His wisdom directs all, and His love and grace influence all the crosses and all the losses of a Christian's state so that they shall work for his good and advantage. Hence Hebrews 12:6: "Whom the Lord loveth He chasteneth, and scourgeth every son whom He receiveth." Now see the design of God in all afflictions, the design that love and grace are managing and carrying on in order that good may result to us from all afflictive dispensations. "For they verily for a few days chastened us after their own pleasure, but He for our profit, that we might be partakers of His holiness" (verse 10). He fans you that He may fan away your chaff. He puts you into the furnace to refine you from your dross and make you purer gold. He is carrying on a design of grace and holiness by all the emptying providences that He brings upon your state, and by all the changes that He makes in your condition. "In measure, when it shooteth forth, thou wilt debate with it. By this shall the iniquity of Jacob be purged, and this is all the fruit to take away his sin" (Isaiah 27:8–9). "And I will cause you to pass under the rod, and I will bring you into the bond of the covenant" (Ezekiel 20:37). They were God's covenant people already; therefore He means, "I will bring you more into the covenant. I will bring you to walk closer to the covenant of My grace." The apostle, under this consideration, tells us "that the trial of your faith, being much more precious than of gold that perisheth, though it be tried with fire, might be found unto praise and honor and glory at the appearing of Jesus Christ" (1 Peter 1:7). This is from the blessed design that Christ Jesus is managing through all your afflictions, in wisdom directing them and in love and grace influencing them. Hence the Apostle James says, "My brethren, count it all joy when ye fall into divers temptations" (James 1:2). Why, how is it possible for a Christian to do so? Let him but consider that infinite wisdom reconciled directs the temptation, and that love and grace influence the temptation, and then, behold, he may count it all joy when he falls into divers temptations. "For our light affliction, which is but for a moment, worketh for us a far more exceeding and eternal weight of glory" (2 Corinthians 4:17).

Hence see how all the losses, crosses, troubles, and temptations of a Christian's state are made subservient unto his main and spiritual interest. They help to perfect holiness that is begun and to bring your hearts closer to God; they cause you to walk more watchfully, to live more believingly and dependently, and to carry yourself more humbly before the Lord. Now, Christian, here is a further ground of rejoicing for you, whatever the emptyings of your state are, whatever the losses and the crosses of your present condition are. Why, say, "Wisdom directs, and love and grace influence all for the best. If I am broken, it is for the best that I should be broken; if I am thus and thus afflicted, why, it is best for me to be thus afflicted. If I am thus and thus re-proached, I will be contented, and I will be satisfied with the will of God; it is best for me to be thus re-proached. If I am thus and thus tempted, I am thus and thus unsettled, thus and thus hurried, God sees it best for me to be thus, so this is the best condition, and this is the best providence; this is the best dispensation for me; God sees that it is so, for wisdom directs and love and grace always influence."

5. Whatever the failures of your outward condition are, Jesus Christ always keeps the wells of salvation open for you; they are always full, and you may come and have your fill. Earthly springs oftentimes run low, but promise streams are always high. Earthly cisterns are often empty and dry, but the promises, which are the wells of salvation, are always full. The leaves and the blossoms of your outward condition are often blasted by the wind and withered by the frost, and they drop off; but the promises always keep their greenness. They al-ways keep their beauty; they always retain their fullness.

Christian, there is a fullness in the promises that you can never draw out; if you should spend all your days upon a promise, you could never empty it. The saints who have gone before us have been spending one age after another upon the promises, and still they are full. And those promises are full with a running-over measure now, whatever your condition is in this world. If you are a believer, there is some promise of grace that suits your condition; whatever your temptation or trial is, there is some promise that offers relief. Whatever your necessity is, there is some promise standing ready with mercy and grace.

Now, Jesus Christ stands at the head of every promise, and keeps the way clear and the passage free for every believer; therefore Christ is called the "Yea and Amen" of every promise. That is, they have their certainty and their stability in Him and from Him, confirmed by Him, and are communicated from Him. Jesus Christ is the Lord of every promise, and He will see, Christian, that you shall not be wronged of your right. He will not allow anyone to come and take away your blessedness that lies there. Now, whatever you lack in your outward condition, the promises are always full, and you may go there for relief. We read that the Philistines filled up the wells that Abraham's servants had dug (Genesis 26:18). These wells of water were stopped; enemies could fill them up. But, my friends, all the devils in hell cannot fill up one well of salvation; they cannot rob a Christian of one gospel promise, neither can they obstruct his way to the promise; for Jesus, who sits above and is at the head of the promise, always keeps the way clear and open.

Now, my friends, here is another ground of rejoicing for you in Christ Jesus. You look into your estates, and you see that you are on the losing hand daily. You look upon your outward condition, and you see that you are going down there. You look upon your outward comforts, and you see them fading, dying, uncertain, perishing before your eyes. Well, but your choicest

blessings lie in the promises, and these are in no uncertainty. Though you do not have a friend upon earth
to go to, and though you do not have a fullness upon
earth to go to, yet you have a fullness in the promise
that you may go to. There is a fullness of mercy and a
fullness of grace in the promise where you may go.
Those who have taken away your outward comforts
cannot take away your comfort in the promise, neither
can they stop up your wells of salvation. Thus, says
David, "This is my comfort in my affliction; for Thy
Word hath quickened me" (Psalm 119:50). "This is the
word of promise that came to my soul with life, and that
was as life from the dead unto me, when I was in a low,
and in an afflicted state; when I was sorely tried and
broken in upon."

Consider, Christians, that you have a ground of rejoicing in Christ Jesus that He is the "Yea and Amen" of
every promise (2 Corinthians 1:20) who can never fail.
He secures the grace of every promise for you, and the
comfort, the light, and the strength of every promise
for you. You may, therefore, though you are brought
low in your outward condition, look up unto Christ
Jesus and rejoice.

6. Jesus Christ is always a light unto the believer in
all his darkness, and a guide unto him in the intrica-
cies of his way unto His Father's house. We know not
which way to go, nor how to direct our own steps; but
Jesus Christ is promised as a Light, as a Light unto the
world. And that is not all, but He is a Light unto His
own people in a special manner, and a guide unto
them in all their ways. "To give light to them that sit in
darkness and in the shadow of death, to guide our feet
into the way of peace" (Luke 1:79).

The believer wants direction, and he wants advice from the Lord, how to steer his course. Jesus Christ stands by him and administers it. He opens the way. He reveals the mysteries of the kingdom. He instructs the ignorant, and teaches those who are fools the great and deep things of God; and therefore the promise is that "the wayfaring men, though fools, shall not err in the way of holiness" (Isaiah 35:8). He will guide them, direct them, and instruct them by His counsel at all times. And because believers go in a wilderness way that is very hard to find, and dangerous and hazardous, Jesus Christ therefore is such a guide who takes charge of them as a Commander and Leader. So the promise runs: "Behold, I have given Him for a witness to the people, a leader and commander to the people" (Isaiah 55:4), importing that He takes charge of the believer in his wilderness way. He directs him in his course, and He will see that he shall be safely guided to His Father's house.

Now, Christian, here is a further ground of rejoicing for you. You meet with many troubles, discouragements, and disappointments in your outward condition. But Jesus Christ will see that you shall not be disappointed of heaven, for He is an abiding light to you, a constant guide to you, and He will so lead you so that you shall not stumble, nor fall, nor perish in your way unto the kingdom.

7. Jesus Christ maintains the union of the believer with Himself, from whence arise unchangeable relations of grace, both between the believer and Him, and between the believer and the Father; and believers may always plead the benefits of this relationship at the throne of grace. My brethren, Jesus Christ takes believ-

ers into a near and intimate union with Himself, and makes them branches of Himself, who is as the stock. He makes them as bone of His bone and as flesh of His flesh. He takes them into a union that He will never allow to be broken. It is an indissoluble union; it is an insuperable and an inseparable union. Therefore, says Christ Jesus, "Those that Thou gavest Me I have kept, and none of them is lost" (John 17:12). Jesus Christ never lost a member. Jesus Christ never lost a limb. Jesus Christ never lost a true subject. Jesus Christ never lost a sheep out of His fold. So this near and intimate union is an indissoluble union.

Now, from this union arise everlasting, unchangeable relations of grace, which believers may always plead as they draw near to God. From this near and intimate union with the Lord, Jesus Christ ever abides as your Head, filled with strength to animate you and to influence you, filled with wisdom and knowledge to instruct and inform you, filled with understanding to guide you in your way. In this intimate union you are members of His body. He will never allow you to be cast off; so you, believer, may always stand in Him, and plead the advantages of a standing in Him, and of an implantation and engrafting into Him. Jesus Christ in this union is always your Husband and you are always His spouse; and the advantages of this relation are always enjoyable and always pleadable. "I will betroth thee unto Me forever . . . in righteousness, and in judgment, and in loving-kindness, and in mercies. I will even betroth thee unto Me in faithfulness; and thou shalt know the Lord" (Hosea 2:19–20). He will never cast you off. He will never give you a bill of divorce. He will be your Husband forever, and you shall be His spouse forever. The relation is always pleadable. And in your near and intimate union with Himself, as you stand in relations of grace to Him, so you stand in relations of grace to the Father; you are the adopted children of God. God, the Father of Christ, is your Father, and He is always your Father, and you are always His children. Nothing can come between; nothing can cause Him to cast you out and disinherit you. Having been received into this firm and intimate union, you are heirs; being made one with Christ, you are joint heirs with Jesus Christ, heirs of God; once an heir, and forever an heir. So that all the blessed things of the purchase of Christ Jesus, and the whole inheritance of Christ Jesus, are before you. They are yours, and for you.

And now, Christian, what a ground of rejoicing is here for you! What if your outward comforts are coming and going, fading and vanishing? It may be that you have your hands full of them today, and tomorrow they will be gone, and you shall see them no more forever. Yet know that you have an abiding ground of joy in Christ Jesus, for it is He who maintains the union with Himself. He has not only united you, but He keeps you in union, and He maintains all the gracious relations of the union, with both Himself and His Father. So that though you may not have a friend upon the earth, you may go and say, "Well, I have a Friend in heaven. I have no father upon earth, but I have a Father in heaven. I have no husband upon earth, but I have a Husband in heaven. I have no faithful brother upon earth, but I have a sincere-hearted Brother in heaven." The relations of grace hold, and a believer may always plead them and make every use of them for his soul's advantage.

8. Jesus Christ is making glorious provision in heaven, and will in due time glorify all His people with Himself forever. So He says, "It is expedient for you that I go away" (John 16:7). "It is for your good; it was for your good that I came, and it is for your good that I stayed so long, and it is for your good that now I go away. For I go to prepare a place for you. In My Father's house are many mansions, and I go to make these mansions ready for you (see John 14:2). I go to heaven as your Forerunner."

Consider Jesus as your Forerunner, who has entered in for you beforehand, making heaven ready, preparing the crown and the kingdom for you. Now, brethren, though you may be robbed of your earthly comforts, you cannot be robbed of your heavenly glory. You may be spoiled of your treasures here upon earth, but you cannot be cheated of your treasures in heaven. Why, Jesus Christ is there to secure it, and He has it in possession. He is there as your Forerunner. He is there to make all ready. "Father, I will that they also, whom Thou hast given Me, be with Me where I am; and may the glory that Thou hast given to Me be bestowed upon them, that they may be one, as Thou, Father, and I are one" (see John 17:20–24). Now, under all your vicissitudes, changes, emptyings, and spoilings in this world, look up to Christ Jesus, see heaven sure in Him, see glory sure in Him, and see a crown and a kingdom sure in His hand. Take comfort then, Christians, in all your necessities here below, in the Lord Jesus Christ, and, with the prophet, always glory and rejoice in Him.

In closing this portion of my remarks I wish to say a sentence or two unto those of my hearers who have not, by faith, laid hold of Christ Jesus, to point out to them how miserable their state and condition is. Why, sirs, you have heard that there is an abiding ground of joy in Christ Jesus for the believer, whatsoever his state is. But do you consider that none of this belongs to you? All this comfort belongs to saints, not to you; you have no part in it. There is an abiding ground of terror, of sorrow, and of bitterness that belongs to you, because you are apart from Christ, who has such a fullness of all joy in Him for believers. Take heed, therefore, how you content yourselves in a Christless state, and how you bless yourselves while you are remote from Jesus Christ, and without a part and interest in Him.

O Christless sinner, you are not under the blessing but under the curse. The flaming sword hangs over your head, and the handwriting is over you upon the wall. Let then the sinner tremble on the consideration of his perishing condition in which he is outside of Christ. And let it be an inviting word to all of you who have not yet come to Jesus Christ, that you inquire after Him, and earnestly pursue Him for your rest and your peace, your comfort and your blessedness. It is all in Him, and can be obtained only by a union with Him by faith.

Chapter 2

The Possibility and Advantage of a Believer, Knowing That He Has an Interest in Christ Jesus So That He May Rejoice in Him

DOCTRINE: There is enough in Christ Jesus alone for the soul's full rejoicing and triumph, whatever his condition is in this world.

Before I come to that which I further proposed to consider and speak to, how the believer should be helped to live a life of faith on Christ Jesus for his spiritual joy and comfort in all conditions, I shall briefly insist upon and labor to clear to you the soul's interest in this Jesus who has such abiding grounds of joy in Him at all times.

The prophet says here in our text, "Yet I will rejoice in the Lord, I will joy in the God of my salvation." I shall insist upon the pronoun "my" in the text ("the God of *my* salvation"), and make plain what is the believer's standing in Christ Jesus, so that you who are believers may know your interest, and that you are indeed united unto Christ Jesus.

It is not in Christ in general, but it is in Christ under or in a peculiar gospel relation to his soul. It is not Christ in general, but in Christ as his Lord and his God that the believer has his interest. And this enables him to rejoice in Christ, whatever his condition.

QUESTION. How may the believer know that he has an interest in Christ Jesus; that this glorious and

blessed Jesus, this full Jesus, is his Jesus, his Savior; that
he may be able to say with the prophet, "Yet I will rejoice in the Lord. I will joy in the God of my salvation"?

ANSWER. Before considering the signs and
evidences whereby you may come to know whether you
indeed and in truth have an interest in Christ Jesus, I
will:

1. Lay down several propositions to you by way of introduction to resolve the inquiry;

2. Show you the grounds and the occasion of the
darkness that is upon the spirits of believers generally
in and about their interest in Christ;

3. Show you what the believer should do in the interim until he can attain to a clear evidence of his interest in Christ Jesus.

4. Give you some discoveries how you may come to
know whether you are indeed and in truth interested in
Christ Jesus.

PROPOSITION 1. In the first place I will point out to
you that Christ is to be enjoyed and rejoiced in only
upon an interest in and gospel relation to Him.

There are many who comfort themselves in a general notion of Christ, that He is a Savior, and please
themselves well with the thought of it; but they will not
find this relieving another day. It is only upon interest
and relation that Christ is savingly enjoyed. It is personal proprietorship and interest that give the soul real
ground of glory and rejoicing in Christ in the worst of
conditions.

A soul can lay no claim to anything that Christ has,
it can lay no saving claim unto any of the sacred blessings that Christ has to dispense, but upon a gospel interest in Him. Neither can the thoughts of Christ be

really comforting unto the soul without respect to this relation that we are speaking of. "But this shall be the covenant that I will make with the house of Israel: After those days, saith the Lord, I will put My law in their inward parts, and write it in their hearts; and I will be their God, and they shall be My people" (Jeremiah 31:33). And Zechariah 13:9: "I will say, 'It is My people'; and they shall say, 'The Lord is my God.' " Here you see a mutual interest and relation; the Lord gives Himself unto His people, and the Lord's people are owned in a near and intimate relation with and to the Lord.

Now this becomes the ground of the dispensing of all the saving benefits of Christ, and the solid and the foundational ground of all the believer's hopes and expectations from Christ. This interest and relation form the ground and visible foundation upon which the grace of Christ is dispensed and the saving blessings of Christ are communicated. Do but see what this interest and relation carry with them: "And I entered into a covenant with thee, saith the Lord God, and thou becamest Mine. Then washed I thee with water; yea, I thoroughly washed away thy blood from thee, and I anointed thee with oil" (Ezekiel 16:8–9). And Ezekiel 34:11–12: "For thus saith the Lord God, 'Behold, I, even I, will both search My sheep, and seek them out. As a shepherd seeketh out his flock in the day that he is among his sheep that are scattered, so will I seek out My sheep.' " You see here the Lord manifests a signal care, and it is grounded upon interest and relation. "They are My sheep," says the Lord, "and therefore I will seek them out, and therefore will I gather them. They are My sheep, and therefore will I preserve them from wolves. They are My sheep, and therefore I will feed them, and lead them into green pastures, and by the still waters." John 17:9–10: "I pray for them. I pray not for the world, but for them which Thou hast given Me; for they are Thine. And all Mine are Thine, and Thine are Mine." "I pray for them," says Christ, "and I will look after them while they are in the world, so that they shall not be devoured and destroyed there." And what is the ground of the prayer of Christ and the care of Christ? Why, "They are Mine," He says. "They were Thine, Father, and Thou gavest them to Me. And now they are Mine, and they are Thine still, and therefore, Father, look after them also."

Interest and relation are the solid grounds of our great expectations from the Lord in all our going to Him and dealing with Him. "I am Thine," said the psalmist, "save me" (Psalm 119:94). And Isaiah 63:8–9: "For He said, 'Surely they are My people, children that will not lie.' So He was their Savior. In all their affliction He was afflicted, and the angel of His presence saved them; in His love and in His pity He redeemed them." And verse 19: "We are Thine. Thou never barest rule over them; they were not called by Thy name." Joel 2:17: "Let the priests say, 'Spare Thy people, O Lord, and give not Thine heritage to reproach, that the heathen should rule over them'; wherefore should they say among the people, 'Where is their God?' " It is interest, you see, that they ground their expectations from God upon.

It is upon a gospel interest and relation that the grace of Christ's fullness, and the sacred blessings and privileges of all His offices, are given out and dispensed unto souls; and without this interest and relation the thoughts of Christ would not at all be comforting nor relieving. But the soul might think on Christ Jesus and be troubled, as you have it in Psalm 77:3: "I remembered God, and was troubled. I complained, and my spirit was overwhelmed." And so a person remembering Christ Jesus, and knowing no interest in Him, must be troubled to think that there is such a glorious fullness in Him, and that he has no right to approach that fullness, nor to expect anything from the all-sufficiency of Christ Jesus. The thoughts of this must trouble a poor creature.

Thus all the blessings of Christ Jesus and all communicable grace are dispensed upon an interest and relation, so that it is of great weight and importance for every one of you to consider whether you have an interest in Christ or not; for if you have no interest in Him, you can have no solid ground of expectation from Him.

PROPOSITION 2. A believer who has an interest in Christ may yet be without the sense of that interest.

Interest and evidence of interest do not always go together; but a soul who is in Christ may be full of fears, doubts, and questionings of spirit in and about its interest. Interest is absolutely necessary to salvation, but the sense of interest is not so. Sense of interest is indeed necessary to our consolation in Christ Jesus, but sense of interest is not absolutely necessary to our safe state in Christ Jesus; for a soul who stands sure in Christ may be in the dark concerning his standing. A soul who is under the everlasting and unchangeable love of Christ may yet be in the dark in and about that love which is glorified, and shall further be glorified upon it and in it. Many a poor believer is just as Hagar was when her bottle was empty and she sat down weeping that now she must die. Why, she needed not to have feared famishing when there was a well of water near her, that she and the lad might drink their fill. True, but she did not know this well of water to be so near her. So the believer's state is safe and good, though he does not know it. Jesus Christ deals with His people as Joseph did with his brethren: he fed them, nourished them, and comforted them a great while, but would not reveal to them that he was Joseph their brother. A believer who has an interest may yet lack the evidence of that interest.

PROPOSITION 3. Evidence of interest is attainable, and it is the will of God that believers should give all diligence to make it clear.

It is possible that a soul may come to see its own standing in Christ Jesus, and know, unto full satisfaction and rejoicing in all conditions, that it has an interest in Him.

Many Scripture saints have delivered it to us upon record that they attained an evidence of their interest. The spouse in the Song of Solomon attained an evidence of her interest: "My Beloved is mine, and I am His" (Song of Solomon 2:16). Job had a clear sight of his interest: "I know that my Redeemer liveth" (Job 19:25). David had his interest cleared up to him: "The Lord is my light and my salvation; whom shall I fear?" (Psalm 27:1). Paul was assured of his interest in Christ: "For we know that if our earthly house of this tabernacle were dissolved, we have a building of God, an house not made with hands, eternal in the heavens. For in this we groan, earnestly desiring to be clothed with our house which is from heaven" (2 Corinthians 5:1–2).

It is the mind and will of God that believers should give all diligence to clear their interest: "Examine yourselves, whether ye be in the faith; prove your own selves. Know ye not your own selves, how that Jesus Christ is in you, except ye be reprobates?" (2 Corinthians 13:5). "Wherefore the rather, brethren, give diligence to make your calling and election sure" (2 Peter 1:10). There is the command, which implies a possibility of attaining it.

The possibility of it appears further in that the Father and the Son have both sent forth the Spirit to be a Comforter and a witnesser to those who are in Christ; and His office is an assuring office. The Spirit comes, being sent forth by the Father and the Son, into a poor heart that is full of fears, doubts, questionings, and misgivings, and settles this soul in the steadfast belief of his abiding interest in Christ Jesus, and Christ's everlasting relation unto it. This you may see: "The Spirit itself beareth witness with our spirit that we are the children of God" (Romans 8:16). "In whom [that is, Christ] also, after that ye believed, ye were sealed with that Holy Spirit of promise" (Ephesians 1:13).

A considerable part of the Scripture is given forth to this end, to clear up a believer's interest in and relation unto Christ, so that he may know his standing in Him. "There is life in the Son," says John, the beloved disciple; "and I write unto you that ye may know that ye have an interest in the Son, and so have life from Him." And this is that which the Lord's people have gloried in (see 1 John 5:11–13). And Isaiah says, "Doubtless Thou art our Father, though Abraham be ignorant of us, and Israel acknowledge us not" (Isaiah 63:16).

This is one end of that grand ordinance of the Lord's Supper, to seal and assure believers. It is not only an ordinance of communion, but it is a sealing ordinance wherein the Lord Jesus comes and sits upon the heart, clearing up the soul's interest in Himself, telling what He has done for it, and sealing all that hath passed upon his soul. It is sometimes hereupon made a feast of fat things. It is an ordinance of joy. It is not a converting ordinance, but it is an ordinance of comfort unto those who are converted, being often owned by the Lord as a sealing ordinance to confirm all that has formerly passed between God and the soul.

It is plain, therefore, that an evidence of interest is attainable, and that it is the will of God that believers give all diligence to make it clear.

PROPOSITION 4. The interest and relation that one believer has with Christ is not different in its nature and properties from what every believer has; rather all who have an interest in Christ have an equal interest in Him.

If you speak of the interest and relation absolutely, they are the same. Jesus Christ is not more one believer's than He is another's. Jesus Christ has not given one believer a greater property in Himself than He has given another believer. But all have an equal interest in and relationship to Christ; all have an equal share in Christ. All have an equal standing in Christ, in point of interest and relation. But if you speak of interest and relation in reference to the use that believers make thereof, and to the effects seen in them, here indeed there is a difference between believer and believer. One believer may improve his relation to Christ more than another; one believer may grow up in Christ more than another; and one believer may, in point of application and enjoyment, possess more of Christ, more of the grace of Christ, than another believer does—but they are all equally interested in and related unto Christ Jesus. And the interest that one believer has is as pleadable and as improvable as the interest that another believer has.

Jesus Christ is equally a Head, a Husband, and a Brother unto all His people; and they are equally members of the same Body in point of interest, though not in point of growth. Hence, says the apostle, "He that is joined unto the Lord is one spirit" (1 Corinthians 6:17). It is spoken in general: let him be an apostle, let him be an eminent saint, or let him be a mean or obscure saint; let him be a strong believer or a weak believer, if he is joined to the Lord, he is one spirit—alike joined, alike related, and with a like interest.

PROPOSITION 5. The believer's interest in Christ is abiding, and can never be crushed; it can never be broken; it can never be violated. But the evidence of interest, though once obtained and seemingly clear, may be obscured and darkened.

A Christian's joy may be passing away and be transient, but his interest is inviolable and inseparable. None can disunite Christ and the believer once they are "gospely" joined. So you have it spoken by the apostle: "Who shall separate us from the love of Christ? Shall tribulation, or distress, or persecution, or famine, or nakedness, or peril, or sword?" (Romans 8:35). "No," he says, "they shall not, they cannot do it." God says, "I will betroth thee unto Me forever; yea, I will betroth thee unto Me in righteousness, and in judgment, and in loving-kindness, and in mercies" (Hosea 2:19). "I know full well what I do," says the Lord. "I will betroth you in judgment. I know what the soul is that I take. I take him so as to keep him and to maintain him. I will hold him and never lose him. I will do it in judgment, and it shall be a relation forever. I will betroth you unto Me forever."

But the evidence of the relation may be clouded after you have had some clear discoveries of it. A soul that is brought into the light may be turned into the dark again. Thus it was with Job. Job had a very clear and full sight of his interest at one time, so that he gloried in Christ Jesus: "I know that my Redeemer liveth." And yet the same Job, at another time, tells us that "the arrows of the Almighty are within me, the poison whereof drinketh up my spirit; the terrors of God do set themselves in array against me" (Job 6:4). It was not the terrors of men, it was not the terrors of his condition, of his poverty, of his sores, or of his great disgrace, but the terrors of God that entered into his soul. And so David, at one time, rejoiced in Christ Jesus, saying, "Though I walk through the valley of the shadow of death, I will fear no evil" (Psalm 23:4), and another time he cried out, "Why art thou cast down, O may soul? And why art thou disquieted within me?" (Psalm 42:11). And in another place he asked, "Hath God forgotten to be gracious? Hath He in anger shut up His tender mercies?" (Psalm 77:9). He mourns after the Lord, and complains as one who was banished from His face.

Though your interest cannot be shaken, Christians, yet the evidence of your interest may be darkened; the love of Christ Jesus for your souls may be so obscured that you may be left without the feelings of it. And the soul that is sometimes under comfortable manifestations, and filled with joy, peace and comfort, may at another time be darkened with clouds, veils, and curtains, and know not where it is. The seal of the Spirit of the

Lord may be so defaced that you cannot tell what to make of it. The believer who is built upon the rock can never be washed off the rock, yet the waves may dash against him upon the rock. He may be sorely dashed upon the rock, though he cannot be washed off. Though your interest stands sure, yet the evidence of your interest is not sure; it is a changeable evidence.

PROPOSITION 6. Sense of interest is in a sovereign hand, and is given out to whom the Lord pleases and when the Lord pleases.

The Lord is pleased to act as a Sovereign in the sealing, assuring, and comforting of His people. Sometimes He will come in upon a believer at his first conversion, and will fill him with joy and gladness that shall abide upon his soul for many years. And sometimes the believer shall wait upon God from ordinance to ordinance, and follow Him many years in the dark, and not have a discovery of His love. Sometimes the Lord will give a soul no sight of its interest, nor evidence of its relation, until it comes to die, while other believers have walked with the evidence of God's love in their hearts almost all their days and then, when they have come to die, have died in the dark. Sense of interest is under a sovereign dispensation, as to the persons to whom it is given out, as to the time when, and as to the way and manner how.

PROPOSITION 7. Though the interest that believers have in the Lord is the same, and is not different as to its nature and properties, yet the evidence of the interest will allow for degrees in different persons, and also in the same persons at different times.

Those who are taken into relation with Christ Jesus are all owned in a near, blessed, intimate relation, as I

told you before, so that there is no difference in the relation, neither is the relation an increasing relation.
Indeed, the benefits of the relation are increasing, but
the relation itself is not increasing. A believer is no
more a child of God afterward than he was at first,
when the Spirit of adoption came upon him; but the evidence of the interest allows for degrees. The relation
itself is capable of an improvement, as to the advantages of it, but that is not all; the evidence of the relation is sometimes clearer, fuller, and more satisfying
than at some other times. It is said that "the path of the
just is as the shining light, that shineth more and more
unto the perfect day" (Proverbs 4:18). A believer has a
little sight of Christ, a glimmering of Christ through
the crevice; this may be improved, and it is possible that
the soul may come into a full assurance of its interest
in Christ Jesus. Yea, and it is possible that you may be
assured more at one time than at another.

Therefore, Christian, the little joy that you have may
grow to a great deal; and the small apprehensions that
you have of Christ may greatly increase in your soul;
and in this respect the day of small things is not to be
despised.

PROPOSITION 8. It is possible that believers may
disingenuously act upon low principles in their earnest
pursuits after sealings and assurances.

I pray, mark it, assurance is the flower of faith; it is
the growth, the improvement, the flourishing of faith;
it is the fragrance, the odor, and the sweetness, nay, the
very brightness of faith. The sealings of the Spirit are
the high strains, as I may call them, of the Spirit in and
upon the hearts of believers. And yet it is possible that
the believer may act upon low principles in his eager

pursuits after the sealings of the Spirit, though it is such a high act. The believer acts disingenuously, in a pursuit after an evidence of his interest, when he presses after the sense of his interest more for peace and comfort than to improve his interest unto more grace and holiness. Your interest in Christ has two streams: the one runs with grace and the other runs with peace and comfort. Now, then, the soul acts disingenuously when it presses more after the stream of peace and comfort than it does after the stream of grace and holiness. The believer acts upon low principles when he advances the sense of interest above the interest, or, if you will, when the desires of the sense of interest outweigh the desires of more grace and holiness upon the interest. Therefore, in all your eager pursuits after the sealings of the Spirit, consider the principle, Christians, upon which you act. Search whether there are any disingenuous actings in your spirits in your eager desires after assurance.

PROPOSITION 9. Satan will indefatigably endeavor to darken your evidence, and to obscure the sense of interest.

Satan's design is to keep souls as long as he can from a union with Christ. He will meet the soul in all ways, if possible, to turn it out of its way; and if he cannot do that, his next design is to obscure its evidence and to darken its sense of interest, so that he may make it walk heavily and in the dark. He will follow you with false reports and false suggestions; he will hint to you this falsity and the other, if possible, to make you believe a lie, deny what Jesus Christ has done, deny your interest and standing in Him which (it may be) is clear upon undeniable grounds and demonstrations. The

devil, you know, came to Christ with this very temptation (Matthew 4:3–6), to make Him question the truth
of His relation to God, though the devil knew well
enough that Jesus Christ was the Messiah, and the true
Son of God. Yet he came and set upon Him with this
temptation, if possible, to make Him question: "If Thou
be the Son of God, then do so and so." He aims at the
believer in the same manner; and his design is to keep
him in the dark, to rob him of all the peace, comfort,
and joy that he might have upon the sense and evidence of his interest.

PROPOSITION 10. There are many who presume
upon a groundless confidence that they have an interest in Christ, and yet are wholly ignorant of the nature
of a gospel interest.

There are many who promise themselves great
things in and from Christ Jesus, and yet they are wholly
ignorant of Him. They have hopes of large blessings
that are to come in by Christ, and yet are ignorant of
Christ, and the nature of union with Christ that gives
them a right to Him. Doubtless, the foolish virgins had
hopes that were as large and as promising as those of
the wise virgins. They never at all questioned their ad-
mittance when the Bridegroom should come, like the
self-deceiver of old: "And it shall come to pass when he
heareth the words of this curse, that he bless himself in
his heart, saying, 'I shall have peace, though I walk in
the imagination [or stubbornness] of mine heart' "
(Deuteronomy 29:19).

So, when we are discoursing of the terrors of the law
that belong to persons who have no interest in Christ,
there are many who bless themselves in their hearts,
and say, "These things do not apply to us." And when

we are opening the comforts that believers have in Christ, those who are strangers to Christ will presume and say, "All these are mine." Micah 3:11: "The heads thereof judge for reward, and the priests thereof teach for hire, and the prophets thereof divine for money; yet will they lean upon the Lord, and say, 'Is not the Lord among us? No evil can come upon us.' " In the midst of all their wickedness, they would still presume upon an interest in the Lord, and think all should go well with them.

My friends, what do you think of the church of Laodicea? They were a people of a very great and high profession; they stood in a gospel body and lived under the enjoyment of the great privileges of a gospel state, and they promised themselves that all was well with them. Yet see what the Lord said: "Because thou sayest, 'I am rich, and increased with goods, and have need of nothing'; and knowest not that thou art wretched, and miserable, and poor, and blind, and naked . . ." (Revelation 3:17). They had taken a profession upon them, and they thought there was a great deal in that. They were in a church state, and they thought that would serve their turn; they enjoyed church privileges, and they thought that, because of it, their condition was good, and that they might well say, "Now we are rich; we are professors in a church state; we are under the common and sacred blessings of the gospel, and who are better than we? We are rich." But the Lord says, "You say so, but I say otherwise. You say you are rich, but I say you are poor. You say you are full, but I say you are empty. You say you are increased with goods and have need of nothing, but I say you have nothing and have need of all things."

Verily, my friends, this is an age wherein many deceive not only others, but their own souls. And, therefore, it concerns you to inquire whether the Lord is your God or not, and not to satisfy yourselves with general notions of the Lord's being your God.

PROPOSITION 11. An evidence of interest obtained, maintained, and "gospely" managed will be of singular advantage to a Christian in his whole Christian course.

You do not know, believers—you who are careless in and about coming to a clear understanding of your state before God—what a change a gospel sight of your interest in Christ will make in your hearts. An evidence of your interest will expel all your fears, will resolve all your doubts, and will cause a calm in your hearts, whatsoever the present storm is. Why, if we could look into the hearts of many, or most of us, I believe they would be found very tempestuous: storms threaten, sore fears are ready to overwhelm, and doubts are even ready to swallow up a Christian.

Why, Christians, an evidence of your interest will remove all these; an evidence of your interest will make all in Christ Jesus precious to you, and will wondrously raise and enhance the price of Christ, and the blessings of Christ in your esteem. The evidence of interest, oh, how precious will it make the blood of Jesus to you! Oh, how precious will it make the death of Jesus to you! Oh, how precious will it make the life of Jesus to you! Oh, how precious will it make the offices of Jesus to you! When you can see that you are concerned in His blood which He has shed for you, that Jesus is your Surety, your Mediator; that He has suffered for you and satisfied for you, that He is your Forerunner in heaven—all will make Christ exceedingly precious.

An evidence of interest will carry your souls cheerfully through all sufferings that do or may befall you in the ways of Christ. There are reproaches that believers meet with in the ways of Christ, and the sense of interest will help you bear them all. There are great losses that we are exposed to in bearing our testimony to the truths of Jesus, and a sense of interest will bear you up under all. Why, we have a building of God that is above. It is said of some in the epistle to the Hebrews that they did not regard their outward comforts, knowing that they "had in heaven a better and an enduring substance" (Hebrews 10:34).

A sense of interest will bear you up under all changes of providences, when the Lord is taking as well as when He is giving. "Why," the soul will say, "there is still enough in Christ. Christ is still full; my Jesus is full. Though I am robbed, He is not robbed; though I have little or nothing, Jesus Christ has all; and Christ is all, and all His fullness is mine."

A sense of interest will raise your hopes and expectations upon Christ Jesus. Now we look upon Christ and have low thoughts of Him; we look upon Christ and our expectations are not raised upon Christ; we come to an ordinance where Christ is revealed and displayed in the riches of His death and in the glories of His life, and our hearts are not raised upon this. Why? Because we do not have the sense of our interest. The sense of interest will raise your expectations, and will comfort you against the thoughts of death. "Lord," said good old Simeon, "now lettest Thou Thy servant depart in peace, for mine eyes have seen Thy salvation" (Luke 2:29–30). And, says the apostle, "I desire to depart and to be with Christ, which is far better" (Philippians 1:23).

The sense of interest will preserve you from all fears of the approaching judgment. Instead of being afraid of it, you will long for the time when the soul comes to see and know and be assured that the Judge of the court is his Friend, is in relation to him, has loved him so as to lay down His life for him, and has ever been designing upon him in a way of love and grace. This soul will not be afraid to appear before Him, but will long for the day when he shall come to see his Jesus clothed with glory.

Thus we see that a clear evidence of interest in Christ obtained, maintained, and "gospely" managed will be of singular advantage unto a Christian in his whole Christian course.

Chapter 3

Considerations as to the Reasons for Some
Believers Being in Darkness Concerning
Their Interest in Christ Jesus

We shall now proceed to consider what the grounds
are of a believer's darkness about his interest in Christ
Jesus.

QUESTION. If there are such solid and substantial
grounds of joy in Christ Jesus for the believing soul at
all times and in all conditions, what is the reason then
why believers are so often in a dark, dubious, uncomfortable, shattered state; that they are seldom able in
any steadfastness of spirit to look up unto Christ Jesus
and glory in Him?

ANSWER 1. The darkness of the believer's interest
often arises from looking more unto such things in the
examination of himself as argue the *height* of an interest
than to such things as reveal the *truth* of an interest.

A believer is apt to fix upon such things as are discoveries of a grown state in Christ, whereas he should
fix upon such things as discover a being *in* Christ. He
proposes to himself that corruption must be so brought
under, and mortifying work must be carried on to such
a height, or else he can have no grounds of an interest
in Christ. He proposes to himself such a measure of
love as must be flaming to Christ at all times, or else he
thinks he has no love at all. He thinks he must have

such a measure of faith so as to believe without staggering, or else he has no part in Christ. Now, hereby he ensnares his own spirit and increases his darkness. But you should look more at such things as argue the truth of an interest than at those things that argue the growth and improvement of that interest.

ANSWER 2. Darkness of evidence often arises from the believer's viewing his wants and overlooking his present receipts. Jesus Christ has done a great deal for him, and has made a wonderful change in him. He cannot deny it if he is but put to it; but he overlooks all this and considers his present wants, his weaknesses, his shortcomings, his failings, his smallness of strength, his staggering before a temptation, the uncertainty of his spirit in his walking with God, and he bears the stress of his condition upon his present wants, not considering what Jesus Christ has already done, nor considering that the work is gradually carried on. Now, Christians, if you would lay yourselves fair for the Spirit's gospel evidence in your soul, then you must take in the encouragements of your condition as well as your discouragements. You must insist not only upon your discouragements, but consider also what Jesus Christ has done, and what a change He has begun to work, and what the movings of your soul have been towards Him from divine influences on your spirit.

ANSWER 3. The darkness of evidence, or obscurity of interest, often arise from the prevailings of sin in the heart, upon which Christ suspends such. Sin rallies and gathers headway in the soul. It presses forward, and the soul gives way to the temptation and is overcome, and upon it darkness arises. This was David's case. David was assured, but sin prevailed in his heart and drove him into the dark, so that all the joys of the Holy Spirit were for a time taken from him. "And Nathan said to David, 'Thou art the man. Thus saith the Lord God of Israel, "I anointed thee king over Israel, and I delivered thee out of the hand of Saul . . . . Wherefore hast thou despised the commandment of the Lord, to do evil in His sight?" ' " (2 Samuel 12:7–9). "I have done all this for you," said the Lord, "and you have despised My commandment and done evil in My sight." So the Lord Jesus speaks unto the soul: "I have thus and thus manifested Myself to you. I thought it not too much to take you into communion with Myself. I thought it not too much to favor you and to give you the assurance of all that I have done for you. But you have wickedly departed from Me and broken My commandments." Therefore it is just with the Lord now to suspend His favors. Prevailings of sin will always cause a suspense of Christ's comforts. You know that Absalom, upon his rebellion, was excluded for a while from his father's house; he could not see his father's face. Just so it is with a believer when he has turned aside into some way of folly; after he has provoked the Lord, the Lord hides Himself from him. He will not let him see His face. The believer may not come into His presence to see Him, and to rejoice in the light of His countenance, as formerly he had done. The prevailings of sin after grace many times cause a suspension of Christ's comforts.

ANSWER 4. Darkness of evidence is occasioned from the believer's crediting the reports of Satan that lead him to deny what Jesus Christ has done for him and in him, upon undeniable demonstrations of the power of His grace in his heart.

Satan will be always putting the soul forward to entertain hard thoughts of God, and will be making false reports in the heart, contrary to the experiences that the soul has had. Now, if the soul will take up a report of Satan, against a clear and visible demonstration of grace upon the heart, and will join with Satan and say, "Aye, this is true; nothing has passed upon my soul. Christ has not loved me. Christ has not taken me nigh unto Himself, neither has He in truth and reality done anything yet for me"—upon the believer's thus falling in with and arguing upon the reports of Satan, he helps to darken his own state and to cloud his interest. Satan is indefatigably industrious to obscure our interest and keep us in the dark. Now he will always stand by you, and be always speaking to you, if he sees that his testimony is received and credited. Therefore, beware how you harken unto him who is ever an enemy unto your interest, and unto your sense of interest.

ANSWER 5. Darkness of evidence arises from our frequent neglects of the Spirit, both in a way of duty and also in a way of comfort.

The Spirit of the Lord attends us, and He is calling us up to obedience, and spurring us forward to closer walking with God in obedience to His commands. Now, when the soul refuses to comply with the Spirit, and does not observe His voice nor obey His commands, but is silent unto His earnest motions in it, upon this is the soul more and more darkened. For the Spirit hereupon withdraws, when we refuse His aids and assistances in the duties unto which we are called. He offers us His help to stand by us, to lead us, and to strengthen us; and we refuse His help and venture upon duties in our own strength, not resting upon Him for strength and power—and the Spirit is hereby provoked. Or we neglect Him in a way of comfort: He would make clear our condition to us, but we will not believe what reports He places in our hearts; He would settle us, and we will not be settled. He offers us consolation, and we refuse His consolation and yet complain of our darkness.

"Are the consolations of God small with thee?" (Job 15:11). Why, the consolations of the Lord are small with many souls; for they refuse them, and they think they do well to refuse the comforts that are offered them, and yet they mourn over their want of comfort. Hereby they grieve the Spirit, they wound the Spirit, and they quench the Spirit—and it is not likely then that the soul should be assured. You have these expressions in Scripture: "And grieve not the Holy Spirit of God, whereby ye are sealed unto the day of redemption" (Ephesians 4:30). "Quench not the Spirit" (1 Thessalonians 5:19). "But they rebelled and vexed His Holy Spirit; therefore He was turned to be their enemy" (Isaiah 63:10). Why, my friends, this is often our case. We rebel against and vex the Holy Spirit of God, and He becomes our enemy, that is, He ceases to comfort us, to settle us, and to establish us. He ceases to fill us with joy and with comfort in and about our interest.

ANSWER 6. Darkness of evidence oftentimes arises from, and is occasioned by, remissness in holy duties, wherein God usually manifests Himself unto us—for example, when we neglect our spiritual watch and lie under or act under the weight of spiritual sloth, deadness of heart, carelessness and flightiness of spirit in our waitings upon God.

This was the spouse's case, who said, "I have put off my coat; how shall I put it on? I have washed my feet, how shall I defile them? My beloved put in his hand by the hole of the door, and my bowels were moved for him. I rose up to open to my Beloved, but my Beloved had withdrawn Himself" (Song of Solomon 5:3–6). Acts of communion were not ceased; the spouse did not decline duties and ordinances, but grew remiss, sluggish, and careless in the duties of communion. She had put off her coat and she could not put it on. Her beloved knocked, but she could not open to him directly; she must make him wait a while. Here were some workings of heart, and some genuine affections in the spouse towards Christ, for she said, "My beloved put in his hand by the hole of the door, and my bowels were moved for him." There were some movings of heart towards Christ, but she moved slowly and was careless in her spiritual frame. And, behold, she looked and her beloved was gone! Here was a suspension, and darkness grew upon her condition. My friends, this is often our case. We let the fire of the altar of our hearts go out and our affections grow dead, and we lose our spiritual fervency; we lose the spiritual favor of communion with God in ordinances of communion, and Christ Jesus withdraws. There is a suspension of manifestations of favor, and darkness increases.

ANSWER 7. Darkness of evidence sometimes arises from unkind and unworthy jealousies of the love of Christ's heart for us, notwithstanding long strivings with us.

The believer does not know how to trust that Jesus Christ is in earnest with him; when it comes to his own particular case, then he entertains hard thoughts of Christ. "Oh, surely Christ does not mean me! Surely Christ is not in the way of grace with me!" Although he cannot deny, being put to it upon a serious examination, that there is a strange alteration in his soul, yet he is always questioning the truth of Christ in His way to him. Not but that he believes Christ is in good earnest in the design, but he does not know how to believe that Christ Jesus is really engaged in a design of love upon his heart. He thinks that the proposals which Jesus Christ makes are not in good earnest, that He does not mean him; that Jesus Christ overlooks and passes by his soul, and that it is others that He is seeking after, and others that He is designing upon. And by these unworthy jealousies, he provokes Jesus Christ. And it is just with Christ to leave the soul a while to itself that will not be persuaded to have good thoughts of Him.

ANSWER 8. Darkness of evidence sometimes arises from, and is occasioned by, our failure to consider the present state of our own hearts, and our inattention to what has passed upon us.

There is a work wrought in the believer, but he has not been so wise as to observe the motions of Christ Jesus in His coming in and in His dealings with him. He has not kept an account of the doings of God with him, but has been very remiss in the observance of the state of his heart as he has passed on in the way, following Christ and waiting upon Him in ordinances. And hence he can make nothing of his condition; he cannot say that the work of grace is so wrought in him in a certain way because he has not been observant to gather up what has passed upon his spirit.

ANSWER 9. Darkness of evidence sometimes arises from unbelieving fears.

There is a kind of "ungospel" modesty that some Christians express, wherein they would discover a great deal of unworthiness in themselves, and a great deal of lowliness of spirit; but in it they only deny what Jesus Christ has done, and wrong their own case. They cannot tell how to believe that Jesus Christ has been dealing with them, and has made powerful applications of His blood unto them, and has united and reconciled them unto Himself; they can hardly think this of themselves. "An interest in Christ is a great thing, and a heart change is a mighty change. I dare not think," says the soul, "that the Lord has done this for me, who am so vile and so unworthy." And thus the soul stands and reasons and denies its comforts.

ANSWER 10. Darkness of evidence sometimes arises from peremptory conclusions as to our state, upon the reports that sense makes when we look at our feelings.

The reason for our darkness is that we lay the stress of our condition upon sense, and upon what we can feel in ourselves, and not upon a simple venture upon Christ Jesus; not upon a gospel-throw upon Christ Jesus, whatever be the issue. The soul goes to its feelings, and makes a judgment of its state upon and from them. When a man can find his heart warmed for Christ, when he can find his spirit under any gospel enlargement for Christ, when he can find his graces begin to grow and thrive, and when he can find speedy returns made unto all his seekings after the Lord, then he concludes, "Now all is well; here is an interest, and behold the fruits of it." But now, when the soul's graces are a little clouded, when he misses that enlargement which sometimes he has experienced, when he comes under some difficulty, and when Jesus Christ is for a while silent unto his prayers, why, then, he concludes against himself: "Oh, there is no interest! Why, if I were in Christ Jesus it would be otherwise with me. Christ would answer me, Christ would enlarge me, and Christ would heighten and brighten my graces. Christ would not leave me in such an uncomfortable condition. He would fill me, lift me up, and set me on high! Oh, surely there is nothing of truth and reality that has passed upon my soul!"

Now, Christians, while you draw up peremptory conclusions as to your state, upon the reports of sense in your hearts, you will never come to be settled and established while you are in this world. Conclusions drawn from changeable, mutable principles will never be relieving nor comforting to you.

Well, these things thus briefly set forth may suffice to explain what may be the grounds of a believer's darkness in and about his interest in Christ Jesus.

Chapter 4

Earnest Directions to a Believer While in the Dark Concerning His Interest in Christ Jesus

Having shown that Christ is to be enjoyed only when the soul knows of its interest in Christ, and having pointed out some things that are occasions of darkness to believers in regard to their interest in Christ, we shall proceed to answer this question:

QUESTION. If it is so that believers are oftentimes in the dark in and about their interest, and have no clear evidence of their relation to Christ, what should the believer do in the interim until the Lord shall be pleased to reveal and unfold Himself to him, and seal and confirm all that He has done for him and bestowed upon him?

ANSWER. There are ten particulars that I shall lay down here in the way of direction.

1. In case of darkness of evidence, strengthen the direct act of faith.

There is a direct act of faith and a reflex act of faith. The direct act of faith is an act of laying hold of, a trusting in, a leaning upon, in short, an act of complete reliance upon Jesus Christ. The reflex act of faith is the believer's glorying and triumphing in Christ Jesus, with whom he has already closed.

Now, Christian, if you do not have the assuring act of faith, then be sure that you strengthen faith in its closing act, and in its believing act, wherein it rests on Christ Jesus alone. Go more often unto Christ, and there fix your soul; resolve ever to wait upon Him and to abide at His footstool. The believing act of faith, or the direct act of faith, I may call the first act; and the reflex act of faith, I may call the second act of faith. Now, Christian, if you are not able to come up to the second act of faith, then be often repeating the first act of faith. Be often resting your soul upon Christ Jesus, and by this means you may come to be assured. For the direct act of faith has a tendency in it to carry you up unto a full assurance in Christ Jesus; and therefore be often repeating that act. You do not know how soon the joy of your assurance may come in.

In case of darkness of evidence, take notice of and rejoice in the strengthenings and upholdings of the Spirit, though for the present you are without the sealings and assurances of the Spirit.

Let it not be a small thing unto you that though you are not comforted, and though your interest is not made clear, yet you are kept waiting upon God. Who is it that upholds you against all your discouragements? Could you hold out by yourself? Could you bear up when there seem to be no returns made, and when there are nothing but discouragements in your way? You cry again and again, and have no return but a seeming repulse. Who is it, do you think, that upholds you? Doubtless it is the Spirit of the Lord. Who upheld the woman of Canaan when Christ Jesus chided her and seemed to give her a repulse? Doubtless, while He seemed outwardly to discountenance her, He was secretly upholding and drawing her heart nearer to Himself, or else she would have fainted. Now, if you have had a heart to continue waiting upon God, and your desires and resolutions are still to follow the Lord, take notice of these upholdings of the Spirit, and bless God for them, and it may be that the Spirit, in a little while, will go on to assure you.

3. Upon darkness of evidence and want of assurance, labor to heighten true grace and holiness. Strive to increase and to grow in grace, for that will be more to your advantage than to bend your desires wholly for comfort and for assurance.

It is a greater mercy for God to give you a new measure of grace than to give you a new degree of comfort. It is a higher privilege. There is more in grace than there is in comfort, for grace has a more immediate tendency to God's glory; the other tends more immediately to your satisfaction and joy. There is more in a little grace than in a great deal of consolation. It may be that the Lord sees that you are not fit for comfort, nor yet fit for settlement and for peace, and therefore He holds you in the dark. Now, the heightening of grace will fit you for the enjoyment of an evidence. The higher grace there is in the heart, the fairer the soul lies for an evidence; the more grace you have, the more fit you are for the joys and consolations of the Holy Spirit. Therefore strive to heighten grace and holiness upon the lack of an evidence.

4. Keep waiting upon the Lord in your way, though the answer is delayed.

You are seeking to be assured, and you are waiting for an evidence of your interest, and yet it does not come. Well, hold on, Christian, and do not give up until the answer is given. He who believes makes no haste (see Isaiah 28:16). Wait quietly (Lamentations 3:26) and patiently upon the Lord (Psalm 37:7), pressing after Him that He would remember His word from ordinance to ordinance; but do not give up. Know that while the Lord suspends the evidence of your interest, He calls you to abide in a waiting posture. So therefore continue to watch and pray.

5. Diligently attend all revealing ordinances, but limit your desires after a sense of interest, in waiting upon the Lord, to the ways that He has consecrated for dispensing it.

God has been pleased to appoint many ordinances for us to wait upon Him in, wherein He is pleased to make Himself known. Sometimes He does it in one ordinance and sometimes in another; sometimes He will come to us in prayer, sometimes in meditation; sometimes He will come in preaching and sometimes in that great sealing ordinance of the gospel, the Lord's Supper. Now, attend upon the Lord in all sealing ordinances, but limit your desires to the ways that the Lord has consecrated for dispensing it. Do not expect that God will work a miracle to confirm you; do not think that there must be a voice from heaven to settle and satisfy you; do not look for some miraculous expressions or impressions upon you, but set boundaries on your desires after the sense of your interest in His own way. I mention this point because Satan rushes upon many souls here; they cannot believe an ordinary evidence, and a small sign will not serve them but they must have some immediate appearance from heaven, an immediate testimony from heaven, in some miraculous way upon their spirits, or else they cannot think that their state is good. And the design of Satan here is to drive you into such a way wherein you shall certainly meet with a disappointment, and, being under a disappointment, then you may more easily and more strongly question your state. But we are not to expect revelation, nor miraculous operations, but to wait upon the Lord in His own consecrated ways that He has appointed for dispensing pardon, peace, comfort, and an evidence of our interest in Him.

6. Again, look upon and rejoice in the dawnings of the day even when you cannot see the sun in its noonday brightness.

My meaning is that you should bless God for a little, let it be ever so small, that He has given to thee, and hold fast to it with much thankfulness. Though you do not have a full assurance of your interest, yet bless God that you have the liberty to follow Christ. You do not have a full sight of your standing in Christ, but bless God that you have the liberty to cry after Christ. You may cry after Christ, though for the present you cannot rejoice in Christ. Well, if the Lord has given you a heart for this, you should magnify His name. Let the work be ever so small that is in your soul, yet, if you are on the way to heaven, bless God for it.

It is a matter of comfort to you in your present state, Christian, that though you do not yet have assurance, yet you are on the way to being assured; though you do not yet have a full evidence of your interest, you are on the way of following after Christ, and you do not know how soon you may have the evidence of your interest. It is a comfort to a child to consider that, though he is some distance from his father's house, yet he is on the way in his journey to it. So, Christian, though you do not have all, yet you are on the way to more; you are on the way to being assured, and on the way to the full possession of Christ. Take notice of this, and bless God for it.

7. Prefer service for Christ before assurance in Christ, and esteem duty for and towards Christ before consolation in Christ.

It argues a very low and mercenary spirit to act for or towards the Lord only upon the feelings of our interest in Him, or only for the comforts that attend a sensible interest in Him. No, we must follow Christ wherever He goes, and prefer service for Christ before comfort in Christ. We must resolve to follow Christ and serve Him whether He settles us and comforts us or not. It is a very filial, genuine spirit in a child to say, "Well, let my father give me a portion or deny me a portion, yet I will serve him; though my father disinherits me, yet I will serve him." Just so should the believer say; he should prefer a command before a promise, and assistance for duty before recompense for duty. Now, it may be, Christian, that you have failed here; therefore advance your esteem of the command, advance the honor of duty and service for Christ, and let these things be uppermost in your heart, and in due time the Lord may more fully appear to you to settle thee, and to comfort you while you are serving Him.

8. Upon the rising of new darkness, have recourse unto the former experiences that you have had of peace, joy, and comfort in believing.

God, it may be, withholds a new word because He would have you go to the old word that He has spoken before; and God may withhold a new sign because He would have you go to the old sign that He gave you before. Now, in present days of darkness, often reflect upon what formerly you have enjoyed in order to sustain your hope and confidence, and make use of that.

9. Be kind unto all the Lord's mourners who are companions with you in darkness.

I mean, learn to sympathize with those who lack the light of God's countenance. The Lord, it may be, in withholding a sense of interest, designs to make you more sensible of another's condition in the dark, so that you may know how to sympathize with him in his sorrows and tribulations, and to comfort others with the consolation wherewith the Lord has comforted you. Therefore, be kind and affectionate to those who are companions with you in darkness. Pray with them and over them, and express the affections of your soul to them in all your remembrances of them. And in a little while the Lord may lead you forth into the company of those whose hearts are made to rejoice and be glad in the light of His countenance, and in the evidence of their own interest in Christ.

10. If you, soul, are still in the dark about your interest in Christ after narrow and deep searches and inquiries, resign yourself up to the Lord Jesus and stand to His allowance, and be willing to work in the dark while the Lord shall keep you in the dark. Do not be your own choosers and carvers in this thing, but leave the Lord to choose for you. Indeed, we are not to rest satisfied in our spirits without an evidence of our interest because it is attainable, but, as to the comfort of our interest, and the joy and peace of our souls upon the interest, we should resign ourselves up to the Lord Jesus, and allow Him to dispose of our state. This is the way to come to a speedy settlement and assurance.

Chapter 5

---

*How Believers May Know that They Have
an Interest in the Lord Jesus Christ*

I shall proceed unto the next thing proposed, and
that is to give you some signs and evidences of your interest and standing in the blessed Lord Jesus. And, as
we say generally, causes are best known by their effects,
trees are best known by their fruit, and life is best
known by its motion, so interest in Christ is best
known by the effects of interest. And that you might
know what Jesus Christ has done in you, and is doing
for you, consider:

SIGN 1. Upon the soul's interest in Christ a divine
principle of life is infused into the heart by the Lord
Jesus, unto whom the believer is united, which becomes
the spring of his spiritual motions towards Christ and
of his profession of Christ.

Interest in Christ is a life-interest, and there is a divine principle of life that is infused by it into the soul
that becomes the spring of his spiritual motions. This
principle of life is variously set out in Scripture.
Sometimes it is called the new creature. "If any man be
in Christ, he is a new creature" (2 Corinthians 5:17). "A
new creature" denotes life. Sometimes it is set out by
the word "life." "He that hath the Son hath life" (1 John
5:12). Sometimes it is called the divine nature. "Whereby are given unto us exceeding great and precious

promises, that by these ye might be partakers of the divine nature" (2 Peter 1:4).

Now, there is life in the divine nature, and the divine nature infused becomes a life-principle in the heart where it is infused, and is the spring of its spiritual motions. This is set out sometimes by engraftment, as the scion is engrafted into the stock; there is a conveyance of life upon the engraftment, and upon the union. Thus the graft or the scion receives sap and nourishment from the root, whereby it comes to live. Now, says Jesus Christ, in your spiritual union with Him, "I am the Vine, ye are the branches. He that abideth in Me, and I in him, the same bringeth forth much fruit" (John 15:5). Again we read, "And if some of the branches be broken off, and thou, being a wild olive tree, wert grafted in among them, and with them partakest of the root and fatness of the olive tree . . ." (Romans 11:17). Abraham is here spoken of only instrumentally, since God was pleased to own him and honor him to be the father of all believers; but Christ Jesus is principally and effectually the root and the stock that believers are engrafted into. He is the root that both Abraham and all believers stand in and grow upon, and they partake of the sweetness and fatness of that good olive tree. Sometimes it is expressed by an incorporation, as the head and the members make up but one body, and every member united unto the body receives life, spirit, sense, motion, and strength from the head. Now, says the Lord Jesus, "You are all members of My body" (see 1 Corinthians 12:12–27). We are all members of the same body, and so have the same Head; and from thence life, spirit, grace, and nourishment are conveyed into every part. Hence it is that Jesus Christ is called the life of believers; "I live, yet not I, but Christ liveth in me" (Galatians 2:20). When Christ conveys and infuses a principle of life into the soul that has an interest in Him, upon that account He is called a quickening Spirit. "The last Adam was made a quickening Spirit" (1 Corinthians 15:45), that He might give life to all those who are united to Him and have an interest in Him. And this spiritual life that we receive from Jesus Christ is the life of our life, and the very soul of our soul, in all our motions Godward; and it becomes the spring of our spiritual profession, and of all our movings towards God.

The soul that has an interest in Christ is not moved by an artificial spring, but it acts and moves from a life spring, from a living spring, which is the principle of divine life that by its interest in Christ it receives. And this is what constrains the believer; this is what moves and actuates him in all his bendings and inclinings Godward. They who have an interest in Christ desire Christ, and move towards Christ upon a principle of life, so that they cannot be satisfied without Christ. "As newborn babes, desire the sincere milk of the Word, that ye may grow thereby" (1 Peter 2:2). The infant cries after the breast upon a natural principle of life; natural life is the principle of its crying. So does the believer move towards and make after Christ from a spiritual principle of life; and that principle of life which he has received from Christ is the holy spring of all his holy or religious actings.

The believer is not moved merely upon a principle to satisfy and silence his conscience, nor yet to get himself a name to live, to make himself honorable among the people who make a profession of Christ, nor yet upon the account of any secular advantage; but there is a divine spring in his soul of spiritual life that he has received from the Lord Jesus Christ, and this works up his heart to the frame he is in, causes him to move towards the Lord, and makes him dissatisfied without Jesus Christ.

Now, my friends, examine the state of your soul by this. What change is wrought in your hearts? Do not eye your profession so much as your hearts. Consider what work has passed upon your souls. Are you spiritually renewed? Have you received life from Christ? Is such a real spiritual change wrought in your souls as amounts to a new creature? Have you received of the divine nature from Christ? And is there a living spring that moves your souls in all your motions towards Christ? If so, it argues an interest; but if the spring of your motion is from outside you, it is a sign that it is artificial and not living, and so it argues no interest in Christ Jesus.

SIGN 2. Interest in Christ unites concerns together, and may be discovered by reciprocal acts in a mutual interest.

The interest which the soul has in Christ is never alone, but the soul that has an interest in Christ Jesus has Christ Jesus interested in him, so that the interest is mutual. And upon a mutual interest concerns are so united together that Christ and the believer have one concern between them. Christ is interested in the believer's concerns, and the believer is interested in Christ's concerns; the believer concerns himself for Christ, and Christ concerns himself for the believer. The believer is interested in all that Christ is and in all that Christ has, and Christ is interested in all that the believer is and in all that the believer has. The believer has a room in Christ's heart, and Christ has a room in the believer's heart. The believer has a possession in Christ, and Christ has a possession in the believer. So says the spouse: "I am my Beloved's and my Beloved is mine" (Song of Solomon 6:3). The interest is mutual.

"Jesus is my Jesus," says the believing soul. "Christ is my Christ. He is my Savior. I have an interest in His love and grace, and I have an interest in His life, in His power, and in His strength and fullness. And Christ has an interest in me also. He has an interest in my love. He has an interest in my heart, in my strength, and in all that I have and am." And the interest being mutual, uniting concerns together, it may be discovered by reciprocal acts; that is, as Christ makes Himself over to the believer, so the believer makes himself over to Christ. "We love Him because He first loved us" (1 John 4:19). He has set His love upon us, and there will be a reciprocal acting in the believer towards Him: he will also set his love upon Christ.

Christ indeed is the first mover, and so the glory must be given unto Him; but the interest is mutual, and the acting is reciprocal. The Lord Jesus Christ makes Himself over to the believer to be his; the believer accepts Christ when offered, but that is not all. He makes a return unto Christ, devoting himself unto Him, yielding and resigning himself unto Christ to be His, and to walk in His ways. In Ezekiel 16:8, you may see the actings of Christ towards the soul. He says, "I spread My skirt over thee, and covered thy nakedness; yea, I sware unto thee, and entered into a covenant with thee, and thou becamest Mine." There the Lord passed Himself over to the believer. Now there are reciprocal actings in the soul towards Him. "Thou hast avouched the Lord this day to be thy God, and to walk in His ways, and to keep His statutes . . . and the Lord hath avouched thee this day to be His peculiar people, as He hath promised thee" (Deuteronomy 26:17–18). Here are reciprocal acts.

Now, Christian, if you would examine your state to know whether you have an interest in Christ, consider what interest Christ has in you, what interest He has in your heart, what a share He has in your affections, and what a place He has in your life. Is there a kind of sacredness in your heart for the Lord Jesus Christ, in a holy resignation to Him? There is one in the soul that has an interest in Christ. "A garden enclosed is my sister, my spouse; a spring shut up, a fountain sealed" (Song of Solomon 4:12). The soul is under a peculiar dedication to and reserve for its Lord, whom it has devoted itself unto, and is as a garden enclosed.

Now, Christian, if your heart lies open, and there is no sacredness upon it and no secret reserve of it, it speaks sadly for you. But where there is a dedication unto Christ, and if you can find He is interested in you, it is an evidence that you are interested in Him; for we can never move towards Him till He first moves towards us. We can never choose Christ until He has first chosen us. If you can find your heart open for Christ and towards Him, it is a clear evidence that His heart has first been opened to you. All our love for Christ is but the reflection of His love for us. Mary did not call, "Rabboni," till Christ first called, "Mary." So if you find your heart under a dedication to Christ—that He is your joy and delight, and has full rule and liberty in your heart; that your heart is opened, or at least opening, and that there are outgoings of soul in you towards the Lord Jesus—it argues that you have an interest in Him, that He has begun to draw you, and that He has cast the skirt of His grace over you and made you His.

SIGN 3. The soul that has an interest in Christ is brought under the ruling power of Christ, so that it chooses Him to be its only Lord.

That soul has as yet no interest in Christ which despises the government of Christ, which refuses obedience unto the scepter and dominion of Jesus Christ. You know, they are reckoned among His enemies who say concerning Him, "This man shall not reign over us." You have a clear Scripture for this in Isaiah 63:19: "We are Thine." How did it appear that they were the Lord's? Because it was asserted that the Lord bore rule over them. And how did it appear that others were none of Christ's and Christ none of theirs? Because He never bore rule over them, neither were they called by His name. So, then, those who slight and despise the scepter of Christ Jesus, and refuse allegiance to this glorious King of heaven, are none of His subjects, and so have no part nor interest in Him.

But now that soul that has an interest in Christ is brought under His rule; and Christ exercises and displays an overruling power in his heart that brings him unto His feet, and he is enabled to live in a professed subjection to the scepter and kingly power of Christ Jesus. Upon this interest that the soul has in Christ, his spirit is satisfied in His government, he is reconciled unto all His commands, he delights in His dominion, and he freely and cheerfully resigns himself up unto the scepter of Jesus Christ. "Lord," says the soul, "here I am; rule over me." Christ never makes a man interested in Himself without bearing the sway in his heart and commanding the powers of his soul: "Thy people shall be willing in the day of Thy power" (Psalm 110:3). When Jesus Christ makes a willing person—that is, displays the power of His grace, brings home a soul, and gives it an interest in Himself—He subjects the heart unto His government. He makes the soul freely willing to be ruled by His laws and by His authority. No laws seem so desirable unto the believer as the laws of Christ Jesus; no rule, no scepter is so pleasant as the scepter of Christ. And all the commands of Christ are chosen by him as being just, righteous, holy, pleasant, and good. The Christian is reconciled to Christ Jesus in the whole of His gospel government over the heart of the Christian. "My Lord and my God" (John 20:28), said Thomas. These two always go together: my God and also my Lord. And this particular I stand upon, and I gather it out of my text: "He is become the God of my salvation." How shall I know that? "He is my Lord," said the prophet. "I will rejoice in the Lord."

The title "Lord" denotes dominion and sovereignty. Now, the soul that has an interest in Christ rejoices in the dominion and sovereignty of Christ Jesus. "I will rejoice in the Lord. I will joy in the God of my salvation." The inference that is drawn from this Scripture, for our present purpose, is this: The soul that has an interest in Christ will rejoice in the dominion of Christ, or receives Christ Jesus as a Lord, and as a Lord rejoices in and under Him.

There may be much weakness in his obedience. I do not say that he exactly and to a tittle walks up to the rule to fulfill every command of God. No, I know that there is a great deal of weakness in the strongest believer on earth, and through the strength of corruption and the violence of temptation he may sometimes be foiled and borne down; but when he is so, still his heart is right, and he loves the commands of Christ which he cannot come up to, and he honors the rule of Christ, and to his utmost makes way for the sway of the sceptre of Christ in his soul. Though he may be borne down by temptation, yet his love remains full unto every command of Jesus. "I thank God through Jesus Christ our Lord. So then with the mind I myself serve the law of God, but with the flesh the law of sin" (Romans 7:25). "I am borne down," said Paul, "I am overcome, but I do not justify myself herein. Rather I bless God that my heart is secured; my love does not abate. I have not waived a command through my dissatisfaction with it. I have not been disobedient to a command because I judged it unreasonable or was dissatisfied in it. No, but my heart still stands for those commands that I cannot reach in my life." Again, "With the mind I myself serve the law of God." And the apostle says, "For God is my witness, whom I serve with my spirit in the gospel of His Son" (Romans 1:9). So then, you see that the spirit stands clear, and is under a constant and full engagement, though it may be that the life does not display that evenness that it should. "With my spirit," he said, "I serve the Lord."

It may be said in the case of the temptation of a believer, as was said concerning the spouse, "I sleep, but my heart waketh." Thus it is with many a poor soul. He may be brought into a sleepy condition, and he staggers and stumbles in his way; he finds it so difficult, but he still says, "While I sleep my heart awakens." His declensions do not arise from dissatisfaction, but his love is reconciled to the command still, and he honors those precepts that he is not able to come up to.

Now, you who profess religion, bring your condition to this touchstone. If you have a heart that slights the government of Christ, if you cannot bear the strict rule and dominion of Christ Jesus over your soul, and if you have your exceptions against the scepter of Christ Jesus being lifted up in your heart, it is a sign that you do not yet have an interest in Christ. "Thou never didst bear rule over them; they were not called by Thy name" (Isaiah 63:19). I pray, remember that the rule which you despise is the only saving rule, and that power which you refuse to stoop to is the only saving power, the only blessed and blessing power. But on the other hand, if you can find that your heart is open unto the Lord Jesus Christ as He is the Lord, as He is invested with all power, as the Father has given all authority unto Him; if your heart is open to Him, and you love His laws in their holiness and strictness, and His government and rule for its closeness; and if way is made in your soul for the throne of Christ to be set up—it argues that you have an interest in Christ, for those who are Christ's the Lord bears rule over.

SIGN 4. An interest in Christ may be known by the distance that the heart stands in from the power and interest of its former state that Christ Jesus has overturned.

The believer, before his coming over to Christ, was under the rule of another lord, and was in subjection to another interest, to the power and interest of sin, and that interest bore sway in his heart and commanded his life. He yielded up himself a servant to sin, and devoted himself unto the service of sin. The apostle speaks out: "Know ye not that to whom ye yield yourselves servants to obey, his servants ye are to whom ye obey, whether of sin unto death or of obedience unto righteousness? But God be thanked that ye were the servants of sin, but ye have obeyed from the heart that form of doctrine which was delivered you" (Romans 6:16–17). And in verse 20 he adds: "And when ye were the servants of sin, ye were free from righteousness." He plainly shows that they were formerly servants to another interest; they were engaged in the service of sin; they acted in sin as if in service to it. As a servant observes, respects, and obeys his master, so the natural heart observes, respects, and obeys sin. It is his lord; it has the commanding power of the soul. It is a most pleasant service to the sinner; though he will find it a sad service in the latter end, yet it is for a time a most pleasant and a most delightful service. Therefore a sinner's walking in sin and gratifying the lusts of the flesh is called his "pleasure," the "pleasures of sin," for he takes pleasure therein. Oh, it is his meat and drink to satisfy the lusts of his heart, in gratifying this lord that is over his soul!

Now, my friends, your interest in Christ may be discovered by the distance that your hearts stand in from the power and interest of this lord that Jesus Christ has overthrown, and which is a constant enemy to your being and standing in Christ. And that I may help you to make a right judgment of your state in reference to your behavior towards sin, I shall explain to you in nine particulars what this distance is which the believer stands in unto the interest of sin, which Jesus Christ has overthrown in the heart upon His making Himself over to the soul.

1. The soul is engaged in war against sin. There is upon the soul's interest in Christ such a distance from sin, his former lord, that he proclaims war against it and becomes its professed enemy. It may be that the life of a Christian is not at present a conquering life, but it is a conflicting life. "I see another law in my members, warring against the law of my mind, and bringing me into captivity to the law of sin which is in my members" (Romans 7:23). Well, there is opposition for opposition: as sin rises up against him, so he rises up against sin. Upon his interest in Christ, he watches sin as one enemy watches the motions of another. He takes all ways and uses all endeavors to foil and bring this enemy under his foot.

2. *There is opposition to sin in general.* The opposition that is carried on and managed in the heart against sin is general. It is not an opposition in one part only, but it is an opposition that the whole soul engages in, and all the powers of the soul are concerned in it. It is not only an opposition in the conscience, but there is an opposition in the affections as well as in the conscience; and there is an opposition in the will as well as in the conscience and affections, and also an opposition in the judgment. The conscience, the affections, the will, the understanding, and the judgment all declare against sin, and all the renewed powers of the soul enter into a strict combination against the interest of sin. The conscience lays loads upon it whenever it appears, the affections declare against it, the will resolves against it, and the understanding and judgment discover it and witness against it. The opposition that is made to sin is general.

3. *The soul can never again love sin.* In this distance that the heart stands in from sin upon its interest in Christ, the heart, in its most deliberate actings, stands in an ir-

reconcilableness unto it. The opposition that is made is not upon a sudden motion; it is not upon a passion of the soul that in cool thoughts will be called in again, but the soul, in its most deliberate actings, stands in irreconcilableness unto it. Not that the affection will never be enticed over to sin again, nor that love will never be invited over to sin again; indeed, the believer may be overpowered so as to sin, but he will never more be reconciled to sin. His love and affections can never be gained to sin again, for the affections are so broken that the distance will ever remain, and the soul will always stand in and act upon an irreconcilableness to it.

4. *The soul hates all sin.* The distance of the heart from the interest of sin, upon the soul's interest in Christ, is universal with regard to all sin. It is not only alienated and drawn from notorious and gross sins that make a great noise in the world, or against some particular sins that his walking in will turn to his disadvantage; rather it stands at a distance from all sin, from heart sins as well as from life sins, from small sins as well as from great sins, and from such sins as are natural to us from inclination, condition, employment, and the like. The heart stands at a universal distance from all sin.

5. *The soul hates all sin because sin is contrary to the Lord.* The distance of the heart from sin, upon its interest in Christ, is great because it has a contrary nature in it to the interest of Christ in him. He opposes sin not upon a particular account, but upon a general one. He opposes sin as sin since it is contrary in its nature unto the Lord, and to the interest and dominion of the Lord in his soul. And so he will oppose sin while sin is sin, and while there is any sin remaining in him. The distance that his heart stands in from sin is since it has a

contrary nature in it to Christ's interest in him and his interest in Christ.

6. The soul hates the appearance of evil. The distance of the heart from the interest of sin that Christ has overturned, upon the soul's having an interest in Himself, is such as hates sin in the temptation. It not only hates sin when it is committed, and when conscience lays hold upon him for the commission of it, but it sets the soul at a distance from sin in the temptation, while it is a great way off. And hence we are commanded to abstain from the appearance of evil, and the saints hate the appearance of evil. That which looks like a disputable evil the gracious heart stands at a distance from, and that which has a probability in it of being an occasion of sin to him the gracious heart will stand off from. The Christian will oppose sin at a distance, and he hates and watches against sin in the temptation. The heart stands at such a distance from it.

7. The soul chooses suffering before sin. The distance of the heart from sin is such that it chooses rather to suffer than to sin. Nay, it will choose a great suffering before a little sin. It will say, "Lord, anything rather than sin." No burden will be like the burden of sin to the believer, no weight like the weight of sin upon his conscience. And therefore he says, "Lord, I will accept any condition rather than to be driven upon a temptation whereby I shall sin; anything, Lord, except sin."

8. The soul struggles against every invasion of sin. The distance that the heart stands in from sin upon its interest in Christ is such as discovers a great reluctance of spirit, and deep searchings of heart, upon the invasions of sin and the soul's being captured by it. Probably he may be foiled and overcome by sin, and many times against his will he is overcome; but, when he is so, he mourns and weeps, and that bitterly. He does not justify the fault; he does not extenuate the offense; he does not hide his transgression, but his soul breaks out into mourning by reason of it, and that upon the passive captivity of the soul by it when against his will he is overcome. He watches and he strives to keep it under, and yet sin is too hard for him; and whether he will or not, sin sometimes leads him captive and carries him out of the way. But he goes mourning into these captivities, and he groans when he falls into the hands of sin, and when he is at any time taken a prisoner.

Thus it was with Paul. He labored against sin with great earnestness, and yet said, "I find that when I would do good evil is present with me; and there is a cursed law in my members that leads me captive to the law of sin, whether I will or not." He strove, conflicted, watched, and did his utmost, yet said, "I find a law that when I would do good, evil is present." He was taken captive, but he groaned under it. "O wretched man that I am! Who shall deliver me from the body of this death?" (Romans 7:21–24). It was one of the deepest and most sorrowful complaints that ever the Apostle Paul made. And thus we find Scripture saints on record, when at any time they have been overcome and led captive, that it has been a time of great sorrow, darkness, mourning, and bitter complaint to them. Now this is another part of the distance that the soul stands in from sin.

9. *The soul desires not only the pardon of sin, but the death of sin.* The believer, upon his interest in Christ, stands at such a distance from sin that nothing will satisfy him but the death of it. Sin seeks the ruin of grace and the

destruction of the soul; the man who has an interest in Christ stands at such a distance from sin that he seeks, designs, and labors to the utmost to hate sin, and to pursue it unto death.

It is not the pardon of sin that will satisfy a true believer. Let me say this much: if you are at no greater distance from sin than to think that, if the Lord will pardon you, all is well and you will lay down your arms, it is a sign that your heart is not right with Christ. If you have an interest in Christ, you will be at a greater distance from sin than this; the pardon of sin will not satisfy you. If sin should be driven into the secret retirement of your soul, and should there remain among the stuff, yet this will not satisfy you.

The soul that has an interest in Christ is set upon the death of sin as its enemy; and that is the meaning of those Scriptures wherein we are called upon to mortify and to crucify sin, that is, to destroy sin, to be the death of it. "They that are Christ's have crucified the flesh with the affections and lusts" (Galatians 5:24). They are doing it; sin is dying, is being mortifed, and is being crucified; and it shall appear to be wholly dead before long. This is what the soul is set upon—the death of this body of death, the utter ruin and destruction of it. It will not be satisfied that sin is mortifying and dying, but the distance of the heart from it is such that it will not bear the very existence of it. Though it cannot drive out all these cursed Canaanites, to have the land at rest and peace when it will, yet it will maintain the war, continue in the field, and never give up till sin is wholly dead.

Now I beseech you, Christians, you who are desirous to make clear your own state, bring your condition to a trial upon this heading, and examine what the distance is that your hearts stand in from the interest and power of your former state which Jesus Christ has overthrown. Examine the distance that your hearts stand in from sin in these nine particulars. Ask yourself these questions:

• Is the distance you stand in from sin such that you have proclaimed and engaged in a holy war against it, or do you only speak slightly of sin before men and hide it in your hearts?

• Is the conflict that you profess to be engaged in against sin general, or is your opposition against sin only in your conscience? Verily, a natural man will oppose sin in this manner. A hypocrite's conscience may check him for sin; a carnal man's conscience may sometimes wound him for sin, and speak high against it; but is the opposition from the affections, from the will, and from the judgment as well as from the conscience? Do all the powers of the soul engage against it? Do they all combine against sin to bring it under? If so, Christians, though sin yet lives in you, and sometimes prevails over you to your grief and disadvantage, yet you are on the better side and have a promising evidence of your interest in Christ.

• Does your heart, in its most deliberate actings, stand in an irreconcilableness unto sin? It may be that the opposition you are making against sin is only in a passion, or only some sudden motion upon a disadvantage that you have met with in your sinful ways. But consider whether your souls deliberately stand in an irreconcilableness unto sin, and whether your affections are so engaged that they refuse to receive this object because your souls loathe it.

• Is this distance universal from all sin? It may be that there are some sins that you would pick at and be willing to part with, but there are some others of which you are ready to say, "Oh, they are but little ones! Good Lord, spare them." Is the distance your heart stands in the same from sin all sin, heart sins as well as life sins, little sins as well as great sins, those sins that are most natural and that your heart and your disposition most closes with?

• Is your distance from sin as sin, as it has a contrary nature in it to the Lord Jesus Christ, and to His blessed interest in your heart? Then the conflict will be abiding as long as there is sin remaining in your soul.

• How does your heart stand against sin in times of temptation? This, verily, is a distinguishing characteristic of a saint. Those whose hearts are not rightly engaged may oppose sin and speak highly against it when it is committed, and when they have seen the ill consequences and effects of it, but do you oppose sin in the temptation, when it is a great way off? And do you shun, avoid, and flee from the occasions of sin, and from that which may probably be an introduction unto sin? Do you avoid that and arm yourself against it? This will be an evidence to you that you have an interest in Christ.

• Do you choose to suffer rather than to sin? Verily, this is also a distinguishing characteristic of the reality of your interest in Christ. Another man may choose to avoid sin when he is harmed by it, or when he cannot apprehend an advantage to the lusts and desires of his own heart, but the gracious soul that has an interest in Christ stands afar off from sin, and so says, "Lord, any condition rather than sin; any burden rather than the burden of sin; any affliction, any grief rather than sin."

• Do you consider what reluctances are in your spirit against the eruptions of sin, and against the passive captivity of the soul by it? Where the heart is not right, it will have no great reflection upon a passive captivity. Upon an active surrender he may, when he has sold himself to work wickedness, be made ashamed of his folly. But a hypocrite, a false heart, will never deeply mourn for a passive captivity. Rather, he will say, "Well, I could not help it; it was not my fault." And so he will excuse it as Eve did: "The serpent beguiled me. I intended no such thing. I was seduced and overcome." A passive captivity bears no great sway in a false heart, but an upright Christian mourns over sin, however passive he is in the prevailing of it. When he cannot prevent sin, he will mourn over the prevailing of it. It will be his constant grief that he was led captive, and that, when he would have done good, evil was present with him, and that he is overcome when he strives to overcome.

• Last, will anything less than the death of sin satisfy you in your war against sin? The gracious man who has an interest in Christ will pursue sin unto death. Restraining grace will not serve him, and pardoning grace will not do, but he will be for crucifying the lusts of the flesh, for mortifying sin in his soul, for the utter ruin and extirpation of it.

Now, sirs, if you can find these things in you, it speaks for you, and will help you to have a clear understanding of your interest in Christ Jesus.

SIGN 5. The man who has an interest in Christ will prize the least of Christ above the greatest enjoyments outside of Christ.

A little of Christ will be more to him than a great deal of creature comforts; nay, a little of Christ will be more to him than all the world. A little of His grace, a little of His love, a little of His Spirit, a small income from Christ, the least love-token from Christ, the least saving gospel manifestation and discovery of Christ—oh, it is the sweetest discovery and the most blessed enjoyment that ever his soul had!

Thus it was with David (if he is the author, as some people think, of Psalm 73, and Asaph only the penman). He at once overlooked his crown, his kingdom, all the treasures that he had in the world, and the whole world that was before him, and said, "Whom have I in heaven but Thee? And there is none upon earth that I desire beside Thee" (Psalm 73:25).

And so the Apostle Paul said, "I count all things but loss for the excellency of the knowledge of Christ Jesus my Lord, for whom I have suffered the loss of all things, and do count them but dung, that I may win Christ and be found in Him" (Philippians 3:8–9). Christ was more to him than all other things; and verily, Christian, so will it be with you, if your heart is right. A little of Christ will be more to you than all the treasures, pleasures, glories, and enjoyments of the whole world; and you will esteem yourself more honorable with a little grace in your heart than with your house full of wealth.

Bring your heart to this touchstone, and consider what it is that your heart is most set upon, and what it is that will satisfy you. If this world and its comforts can satisfy you without Christ, you have no part in Christ. Nay, if you prefer other enjoyments before a participation in Christ, you have none of Christ. If you have a saving interest in Him, the manifestations of Christ to your soul will be the most blessed of manifestations. Oh, the least bit of Christ will be as life to the dead!

The least love-token, the least intimation of His love, the least saving effect and operation of His grace upon your heart, and the increase of communion with Him—these things will be the life and the joy of your spirit. If you can find it so with you, really and in truth, that a little of Christ is prized in your heart above the greatest enjoyments outside of Christ, it is a sign and evidence that you have an interest in Christ.

It may be, Christian, that you have but a little of Christ in your heart, very little of Him—but a little of the grace of Christ, and but a little of the Spirit of Christ—and you can do but little for Him. But the least experiences of Christ are the sweetest experiences to you, your enjoyments of Christ are the most satisfying enjoyments, and your soul will prefer an opportunity for communion with the Lord Jesus before great advantages otherwise. If it is so with you, it is an evident sign that you have an interest in Christ, and you may take comfort in your present standing in Him.

SIGN 6. The soul that has an interest in Christ is under an overruling influence from Christ that secures the habitual inclinations of his soul for Christ against all contrary invitations and drawings.

Particular acts are not a sufficient, conclusive ground of our state one way or another. A soul that has no interest in Christ may seem choice and singular in some actions, and there may be a seeming lovely, desirable sanctity upon that person; and a soul that really has an interest in Christ may, by the power of a temptation, be drawn into some unbecoming acts. So particular acts are no sufficient ground of an interest, and if you judge by them you may easily be deceived. But he who is really united to Christ is under a divine influ-

ence from Christ that secures the habitual inclinations
of his heart for Him, so that the bias of his heart is towards Christ, and the full purpose of the soul in its secret breathings and inclinings is after the Lord Jesus
alone. It may be that, when the temptation comes, he is
almost staggered, yet his heart stands right for Christ
in the main, in whom he has an interest; and though
temptations may have a great power upon him, yet the
bias of his heart will work through all temptations to
Christ alone.

Thus it was with Paul. There were contrary drawings
in his heart, and the temptations that he met with from
the remains of indwelling sin were very great, yet his
heart under all stood right; the habitual inclinations of
his heart were for and towards Christ Jesus, and this was
the characteristic note of his union with Christ. You
may see it in these words: "For that which I do I allow
not; for what I would, that do I not; but what I hate, that
do I. If then I do that which I would not, I consent unto
the law that it is good" (Romans 7:15–22). The old man
was rising and rebelling in him, and made use of all its
strength and its whole interest in his heart to draw him
aside. So he said, "At that time, when I was under those
shakings, then my heart was in the way of Christ, and I
consented unto the law that it was good; for that which
I did not do was that which I would do. And though I
find a law in my members that was warring against the
law of my mind, yet I delight in the law of God after the
inward man. There is my delight: the habitual inclinations of my soul were not changed nor turned, but the
secret workings and breathings of my soul are towards
the Lord Jesus Christ."

Thus it was with David. He had many temptations

and rubs in his way, and they might have turned him aside from the way, yet he said, "My soul breaketh for the longing that it hath unto Thy judgments at all times" (Psalm 119:20). "As the hart panteth after the water brooks, so panteth my soul after Thee, O God. My soul thirsteth for God, for the living God; when shall I come and appear before God?" (Psalm 42:1-2).

And, says the prophet, "With my soul have I desired Thee in the night; yea, with my spirit within me will I seek Thee early" (Isaiah 26:9). The night season was a dark time, and it is probable that his spirit was greatly endangered at that time by temptation; for dark times are times of temptation, and his soul at that time was almost overwhelmed in the conflicts of his spirit with the divisions of his heart in the night season. Now, he says, "When it was thus darkness about me, and temptation arose upon me, then with my soul have I desired Thee. Then my heart stood clear for Christ, though I could not manifest myself as I would."

Now, Christians, if you would make a judgment of your own state, fix your eye upon your hearts, consider how they stand, and secretly observe the habitual inclinations of your hearts. Do you, as the expression is in Acts 11:23, "cleave unto the Lord with full purpose of heart"? Those who are interested in Christ with purpose of heart cleave unto the Lord. There are not only some good thoughts that rise in their hearts now and then; they have not only some scanty desires after Christ, some sudden motions upon their spirits towards Him, but the bent of their heart is towards Christ; at all times the breathings and longings of the heart are after Christ. Now, those who are under such an influence from above so as to secure the habitual inclinations of their souls for Christ against all contrary invitations and drawings—these are such as have indeed an interest in Christ, and this is the influence of the interest on Christ's part upon your souls.

SIGN 7. A man who has an interest in Christ is so concerned for the cause of Christ that dishonors done unto and dishonorable reflections upon the Lord Jesus Christ bear hard upon his spirit.

My brethren, the soul's interest in Christ is an interest that makes you one with Christ; and the soul will be a sharer and partner with Christ in all His dishonors, in all His griefs, and in all His afflictions. Jesus Christ speaks sometimes of being wounded, of being grieved, and of being offended. Now, he who really has an interest in Christ is offended where Christ is offended. He who is really interested in Christ will grieve over whatsoever grieves Christ, either in himself or others. He will be wounded with that which wounds Christ, will mourn over that which is an occasion or matter of mourning unto Christ, and will bear heavily upon his spirit that which reflects dishonor upon the name and glory of the Lord Jesus.

I remember what was spoken of our Lord Jesus in reference unto His Father, and the concern that He was engaged in: "For the zeal of Thine house hath eaten Me up; and the reproaches of them that reproached Thee are fallen upon Me" (Psalm 69:9). Both halves of this verse are applied to Christ Jesus in the New Testament. In John 2 you may see the first phrase applied to Him: "And His disciples remembered that it was written, 'The zeal of Thine house hath eaten Me up.' " Jesus Christ, you know, came into the temple, which was His Father's house of worship, and there He saw His Father dishonored; there He saw His Father's worship corrupted, adulterated, and defiled, and He saw there great reflections upon His Father's glory and was eaten up with it. His holy zeal and passion for His Father's glory carried Him out beyond Himself, to make Him disregard and neglect Himself: "The zeal of Thine house hath eaten Me up." And the psalmist adds, "The reproaches of them that reproached Thee are fallen upon Me." This you have applied to Christ in Romans 15:3: "For even Christ pleased not Himself, but as it is written, 'The reproaches of them that reproached Thee fell on Me.' " Jesus Christ bore that sin upon Himself that was a dishonor unto His Father, that was a wound unto His Father, and that His Father said He was laden and pressed with, as a cart is pressed with sheaves (see Amos 2:13). He took up this dishonor and reproach and bore it upon Himself. He was wounded for our transgressions. He was afflicted and chastened for our sins. "The reproaches of them that reproached Thee fell on Me." Christ came and mourned over sin, and He expressed the sorrow of His heart for that whereby His Father was dishonored.

Now, the man who is really interested in Christ is so made one with Christ that he has fellowship with Him in His dishonor, in His reproaches, and in all His sufferings. He is a partner with Christ in His griefs; he is a griever with Christ, a mourner with Christ, and a complainer with Christ. If there is anything in his heart or ways that offends Christ, he is offended and disturbed with this as soon as he sees it, and he cannot bear it because it offends the Lord Jesus, with whom he is one. And this is what makes true Christians walk up and down with such sad hearts. What is the matter? Why, there is something that they have seen in their hearts that is offensive to Christ, and they cannot bear it. They do not know how to get rid of it. And there is something in their walk and conversation that reflects upon the honor of the Lord Jesus, and their souls are wounded with it. And as to the sins of others, that which is a reflection upon the name, upon the honor and glory of Christ, lies hard upon their spirits. So the psalmist says, "Rivers of water run down mine eyes, because they keep not Thy law" (Psalm 119:136). And see how the prophet Jeremiah complains of that of which the Lord made a complaint: " 'They proceed from evil to evil,' saith the Lord' " (Jeremiah 9:3). And he says, "O that my head were waters, and mine eyes a fountain of tears, that I might weep day and night" (Jeremiah 9:1).

Hence the saints are called mourners in Zion (see Isaiah 61:3), and we read of those who mourned in the midst of the Lord's people. They mourned sometimes for their own sins, as dishonoring Christ Jesus. Thus did Peter when he had displeased the Lord and was sensible of it: he went out and wept bitterly. Sometimes they weep for the sins of others, because they see that the Lord is so dishonored and offended by the lives and conduct of saints.

Now, Christians, by this make a judgment of yourselves, and bring your hearts to this touchstone. If you stand at a distance from the concerns of the honor of Christ Jesus in the world; if you look upon the concerns of His glory as alien things, which you are not concerned in; and if you are not touched with the dishonors of Christ, and they make no impression upon your spirits—truly this speaks very sadly. But on the other hand, if you find your spirits in fellowship with Christ in all His dishonors; if you find that whatever disturbs, displeases, and grieves the Lord is a weight upon your spirits, and that because it is a weight upon the heart of Christ Jesus, this is some evidence that you have an interest in and are united unto the Lord Jesus.

SIGN 8. The man who has an interest in Christ is restless in all pursuits after Christ until he can compass something of Him.

Christ is the center of the Christian's heart, and he cannot rest outside of Christ, neither can he be long satisfied without Him, but is continually pressing after a sight of, and fellowship and communion with, the Lord Jesus, his heart being, as it were, swallowed up with Him. Lead him unto other things and they will not satisfy him outside of Christ; lead him unto ordinances, and these will not do if Christ is not there; advance him unto all gospel privileges which give him a name and renown among saints, and this will not satisfy him if he does not have Christ Jesus there. Thus it was with the spouse: she had lost her sight of Christ, and even though she still had her ordinances and her privileges, this would not satisfy her. She went from ordinance to ordinance, and from privilege to privilege, seeking Christ. "O, saw ye Him whom my soul loveth?" (Song of Solomon 3:3). And truly I may say of such a heart as is interested in Christ, as Absalom spoke in another case, when he was well provided for and had royal princely accommodations, "Oh, what is all this to me if I may not see the king's face?" (see 2 Samuel 14:32). So, whatever outward accommodations a man may have has who has an interest in Christ, he will still be saying, "Oh, what is all this if I do not have Christ?" He will be restless in his pursuit after Christ until he can compass something of Him.

Now, Christians, examine your hearts by this: if you can sit down with something short of Christ, if you can come to an ordinance and have no communion with Christ in the ordinance, and yet be well satisfied; if you can take up your rest in the privileges of the gospel, without the Lord Christ Himself, it is a very clear sign that you do not yet have an interest in Him. But if no ordinance will please you where Christ is not; if no enjoyment will satisfy you if Christ is away; if your eye is upon Christ in and through all enjoyments, as the only rest and center of your souls—this is a good sign of interest.

SIGN 9. The man who has an interest in Christ makes his preparations and his reformations in his heart, and this it is at which Christ principally looks.

He who is united to Christ looks chiefly at the heart, which Christ looks chiefly upon; and his great care is to have this heart swept, cleansed, purified, sanctified, fitted, and furnished for the majesty of Christ Jesus. Heart disturbances and heart disorders are matters of great grief unto him, because he knows that thereby Christ is displeased. Jesus Christ takes up His abode with the soul that is united to Him. Now, Christ's residence is in the heart, and the soul that is united to Christ will principally look to prepare that room where Christ's residence is to be. The soul will use all means to bring his heart into some gospel order to entertain the Lord Jesus; and all that comes from him comes from the heart. The profession that he makes of Christ is a heart-rooted profession, the change of his life springs from the change of his heart, and the holiness and sanctity that he manifests are from the heart.

Now, Christians, examine your own hearts by this particular also. You make some preparations, you are able to show some reformations, but are your preparations only life and conduct preparations? Are they not heart preparations too? Or is your reformation only a life reformation and not a heart reformation? They who have no interest in Christ may prepare and reform, but they will look only to the washing of the outside of the cup and the adorning of the outward man, not the inward man. But now, if your greatest care is for the state of your hearts, and your utmost diligence is to have them thoroughly reformed and under a heavenly disposal for Christ, to make provision there, and to be fitted in the inward man for communion with the Lord Jesus; and if in all your reforming you first begin there, and carry on outwardly as you are able to succeed inwardly—this is an evidence of an interest in the Lord Jesus Christ.

SIGN 10. The man who has an interest in Christ does not live upon himself, nor upon his own actings, but upon Christ, unto whom he is joined.

He who is brought into union with the Lord Jesus makes the Lord Jesus his all, and leans upon Him and stays upon Him, and not upon anything short of Him. Jesus is full, and he lives upon the fullness of Jesus. He comes hungry, empty, and naked unto Jesus to be satisfied and to be clothed. He rests himself upon the merits of Christ, he confides in the faithfulness of Christ, he leans upon the power of Christ, and he acts by the strength of Christ. He lives in all his whole Christian course upon Christ. So says the spouse in Song of Solomon 2:3: "As the apple tree among the trees of the wood, so is my Beloved among the sons. I sat down under His shadow, with great delight, and His fruit was sweet to my taste." Here Christ was the spouse's all; she got under His shade and there she rested; she fed upon Christ, and lived upon Christ. "His fruit was sweet to my taste." The true believer cannot stay upon any righteousness but Christ's, in whom he is interested. You may see this in Philippians 3:8–9: "Yea doubtless, I count all things but loss for the excellency of the knowledge of Christ Jesus my Lord, for whom I have suffered the loss of all things, and do count them but dung that I may win Christ, and be found in Him, not having mine own righteousness which is of the law, but that which is through the faith of Christ, the righteousness which is of God by faith."

Now, Christians, examine your own hearts by this also. What is it that you live upon? Is it upon Christ or is it upon yourselves? If you can satisfy yourselves with a righteousness short of Christ's, that is, a righteousness of your own, it is a sign that you do not yet have an interest in Him. If you do not go wholly out of yourselves to count all things as loss for Christ, it is a sign that you are not yet interested in Him. If you act by your own strength, and do not look up to Christ for strength, it is a sign that you are depending on yourselves, and that you are not yet in Christ. And if your greatest care is not to please Christ, it is a sign that you are not yet in Christ. Those who are in Christ live upon Him; they do not live upon duties, they do not feed upon bare ordinances, but they feed upon Christ Jesus. They trust only in His righteousness; they eye His merits and consider His faithfulness, and they act in faith upon His offices. They trust in Him, and they have reference to Christ at all times.

SIGN 11. The men who have an interest in Christ will, with boundless desires, be always pressing after Christ, and never think they have enough of Him.

Not only will they be restless in their pursuits after Christ till they can attain to some real knowledge of Him, but there are boundless desires in them after Him, and after more of Him. A little of Christ will not satisfy a soul that is interested in Him; though he has a little of Christ, he will still be pressing after more, and think all that he has received is but little. He must have more of Him, more communion with Him; he must be brought into a higher conformity to Him. He cannot rest with a little of Christ. His desires will be boundless, so that he will always, in his participation with Christ, be still looking forward, pressing after perfection, and reaching and designing to apprehend as he is apprehended. He who is interested in Christ always has a rising, reaching desire in him after Christ. This you may see in Philippians 3:12, 14: "Not as though I had already attained, either were already perfect; but I follow after, if that I may apprehend that for which also I am apprehended of Christ Jesus. . . . I press toward the mark for the prize of the high calling of God in Christ Jesus." What an enlarged heart Paul had! He had come to a very high pitch in Christ Jesus, to count all as loss for Him, and to glory in Him and in His righteousness; and yet, brethren, he says, "I count not myself to have apprehended." He says, "Oh, what have I yet of Christ? What have I received yet of the Spirit of Christ? Oh, how unlike am I yet unto Christ! How unsuitable is my heart yet unto Christ! How little of Christ is yet in my heart! Brethren, I count not myself to have apprehended, but this one thing I do: I am reaching forth." He who is interested in Christ will have noble, genuine workings of heart suitable to his union with Christ; he will always be desirous of Him, and pressing after more of Him, never satisfied with anything that he has. Though he will bless God for the least that he has, yet he will not be satisfied with anything that he has, but will be pressing after more, and his language is always, "Give, give."

Now, Christians, examine your own hearts by this. If you really have an interest in Christ, it will have such an influence upon your souls as always to prompt you to press after more of Christ, to get nearer to Him, to know more of Him, and to be filled with the Spirit of Christ. A little grace, grace enough to carry you to heaven, will not satisfy you, but your desire will be to be made to abound in all grace; your desire will be to be holy as He is holy, and to be pure as He is pure, in all manner of conversation (1 Peter 1:15–16). And you will never stop craving and desiring while there is a corner in your hearts to fill, and while there is room for a hungering and thirsting desire to rise in your hearts after the Lord Jesus. Now, if you can satisfy yourselves with anything of Christ, and sit down with a bare profession of Christ, without anything of Christ in your hearts; if you do not have these holy hungerings and thirstings in your souls after high measures, and full enjoyments and manifestations of Christ—it speaks very sadly; but if there are such boundless desires as we have told you after Christ, it is some sign of interest.

SIGN 12. He who has an interest in Christ values himself, persons, and things, as they are in or have of Christ in them.

He measures all persons and things by their reference to Christ, and he judges that it is Christ Jesus only who makes them differ; and whatsoever is excellent in any person or in anything is from Christ Jesus, and it has no more excellency in it than what it has in and from the Lord Jesus. He does not value himself by his outward enjoyments; he does not value himself by his natural gifts and accomplishments, though they may be very great and large; he does not value himself by his privileges in his gospel state, but he values himself by what he is in Christ Jesus. "By the grace of God," he says, "I am what I am." If he cannot discover the grace of Christ in himself, he counts that he has nothing; and if he cannot find some hopes of an interest in Christ, he counts that he is nothing. He owns and makes reckoning of himself as he stands in and has reference to Christ.

If Paul had judged himself by his gifts, who had greater ones? If Paul had judged himself by his privileges, who had higher ones? But he judges these as nothing: "By the grace of God," says he, "I am what I am" (1 Corinthians 15:10). And so he reckons as to all others: he esteems persons as they are in Christ, and those who have most of Christ in them are most excellent. He loves a poor, mean soul in Christ more than the greatest and richest man in the world outside of Christ. If any persons have more of his love, more of his heart than others, it is those who have the most of Christ in them. The most sincere Christians, the most growing Christians, and the most upright Christians are the persons whom he most loves, values, and delights in. As for all ordinances, he values them only as he meets with Jesus Christ in them; if he does not find Christ in an ordinance, he counts the ordinance as no ordinance. And if a Lord's day passes without some communion with Christ, he counts it as no day to his soul. He prizes the gospel of Christ Jesus so much because it is Christ's gospel, and the truths of the Gospel are so dear to him that he can venture all for them because they are Christ's truths.

Now, Christians, examine your state and condition by this also. What is it that you value yourselves by? Do you value yourselves by your bare professions? Do you value yourselves by your enlargement? Do you value yourselves by your gifts? Do you value yourselves by the name that you have among men? Those who are in Christ do not value themselves thus, but by what they apprehend themselves to be in, and to have received from Christ Jesus.

SIGN 13. The man who has an interest in Christ rises and falls in his spirit according to the sensible manifestations or withdrawings of Christ in his heart.

He rejoices as Christ appears, and he is saddened as Christ withdraws; his joy is coming and going as Christ is coming and going in his heart. An appearance of Christ makes day in his heart, and the withdrawings of Christ make night in his soul. When a curtain is drawn between Christ and him, then he is in the dark, and then his soul sits in sorrow; then he is covered over with mourning. But, upon the return of Christ, his soul leaps within him, and he is filled and satisfied as with marrow and fatness. "I will rejoice in the Lord, my soul shall be joyful in my God" (Isaiah 61:10). Why so? Because Christ appears, puts on me something of His own clothing, and gives out something of Himself to me. He comes as a Bridegroom, decks himself with ornaments, makes me as His bride, and decks me with His jewels. Now, this causes me to rejoice in the Lord, and makes me joyful in my God.

Days of communion and seasons of manifestation are the festival days that the believer's soul enjoys, and nothing causes so great a damp upon his heart as when Christ withdraws. This was seen in David. He rose and fell in his spirit as the manifestations or the withdrawings of Christ were there. "Lord," said he, "Thy lovingkindness is better than life" (Psalm 63:3). Ay, there was his joy and gladness. And "Lord," said he at another time, "Thou didst hide Thy face, and I was troubled" (Psalm 30:7); there was his sorrow for Christ's absence. And, said the spouse, "Let Him kiss me with the kisses of His mouth" (Song of Solomon 1:2). By "kiss" is meant some visible manifestation of Christ unto the soul, some discernible token of His love. "Let Him kiss me with the kisses of His mouth; for Thy love is better than wine." Wine was to be given to those who were of a heavy heart, by Solomon's direction (Proverbs 31:6), and in the Psalms (104:15) we read, "Wine that maketh glad the heart of man, and oil to make his face to shine." That wine was to be given to those who were of a heavy heart; because it is that which makes joyful and exhilarates the spirit. Now, says David, "Lord, Thy love is better than wine." There is more in a little communication of Christ Jesus than in the greatest refreshment and heart-cheering in the world; for this love that is better than wine is not love simply considered, but the effects of love in gracious manifestations. John 14:21–22: "He that hath My commandments, and keepeth them, he it is that loveth Me; and he that loveth Me shall be loved of My Father, and I will love him, and will manifest Myself to him. Judas saith unto Him, not Iscariot, 'Lord, how is it that Thou wilt manifest Thyself unto us, and not unto the world?' " This love was a love of manifestation. Now, said the spouse, "Let Him kiss me with the kisses of His mouth." Let love be manifested, and this manifesting love is better than wine. Oh, it will make all other things dainties to him, and will make sweets seem bitter in his spirit. This is sweet indeed, and an abiding ground of joy and comfort to his soul upon the evidence of His love, and upon the sight of His face and communion with Him.

Now, Christians, examine your hearts by this. If your joy is fixed upon something else than Christ, and if the withdrawings of Christ do not cause the greatest sadness unto your spirits, it is a clear sign that you have no interest in Christ. But now, where Christ Jesus is looked upon as the very joy of your souls, and you most of all joy in His presence, and you are most of all troubled at His departure and at the hidings of His face, it is a sign of interest.

It is a sign that a woman entirely loves her husband that she cannot bear that he should be absent from her for long, and is most of all pleased in his company. So it is a sign that the man is married unto Christ Jesus who cannot bear Him to withdraw, and is never so much troubled, tossed, discomforted, and afflicted in his spirit as when Jesus Christ stands behind the curtain and refuses to answer his soul when he is crying after Him.

SIGN 14. The man who has an interest in Christ has constraining, abiding endearments in his heart unto Jesus Christ, so that no discouragement shall turn him off from Christ, but he will cut the way through all opposition to come to enjoy Him.

My friends, if you are really interested in Christ, and

have tasted how gracious the Lord is, difficulties in your way to Him will be no difficulties so long as you may enjoy Him. The soul in Christ will be contented to be reproached for Him so that he may enjoy Him; and the reproaches that he meets with in the way of Christ will be no great matter to him as long as Christ and he may keep together. You may see what was the spirit of an Old Testament saint in Hebrews 11:24–26: "By faith Moses, when he was come to years, refused to be called the son of Pharaoh's daughter, choosing rather to suffer affliction with the people of God than to enjoy the pleasures of sin for a season, esteeming the reproach of Christ greater riches than the treasures in Egypt."

Persecutions will not part Christ and the real, sincere Christian, but though he is persecuted for His sake, yet if Christ and he can but keep close together, he will think all is well. "Who shall separate us from the love of Christ? Shall tribulation, or distress, or persecution, or famine, or nakedness, or peril, or sword?" (Romans 8:35). Why, he says, we can bear all this for Christ. We can bear tribulation, distress, persecution, famine, nakedness, peril, sword. "Lord, anything rather than to lose Thee," says the sincere Christian. He will suffer losses for Christ rather than lose Him. "Lord," said the disciples, "we have left all for Thy sake." And it is said of the primitive Christians that "they took joyfully the spoiling of their goods." Let men frown, let devils frown, still the heart of the sincere Christian will be working Christward, and he will have constraining, abiding endearments in his heart that will cut through the difficulties of his way. He will be willing to lose anything rather than lose the Lord. This is the frame of a soul interested in Christ when he is committed to Him.

I am sensible that an honest heart may be suddenly surprised by the strength of a temptation as Peter was; but it will be but for a moment, and he will rise again. He will not quit his interest in Christ, nor will he sell his part in Christ. When he comes to reflect and consider that Christ and he cannot live asunder, his interest in Christ will have such an influence upon his soul as will cause him to abide in the Lord, so that, whatsoever he meets with, yet he desires above all to enjoy Christ. He will go through fire and through water, if that is the only way that the circumstances of divine providence permit him to enjoy Christ. I pray, mark the connection in Philippians 1:29: "It is given to you to believe, and also to suffer." Upon the soul's believing, its interest is united with Christ, and it is one with Christ. Now, said the apostle, those who believe, that is, those who have an interest in Christ, will also suffer for the sake of Christ. And the same power that helps them to believe also bears them up against the frowns and the discouragements that they meet with in the way of Christ.

Well, Christians, examine your own state by this particular. Do your hearts stand affected and endeared to Christ in a day of suffering, when difficulties look you in the face, when reproaches are likely to befall you, when losses and injuries in your outward condition are likely to come upon you? Can your hearts say, "Whatsoever comes, oh, let us have Christ, for He is more than all"? And whatever we enjoy in Christ is more than we can lose for Him!

There is a constraining, abiding endearment in the heart that is really united to Christ, and it will cut the way through all opposition. It is not thus with one who has no interest in Christ. The young man in the gospels made a very fair profession of Christ, and came and pretended to be His most forward disciple. But Christ said to him, "Can you live upon Me alone? Can you suffer anything for the enjoyment of Me? Will you value and prefer an interest in Me before all your possessions?" "No, Lord," said he, "I have great possessions. What! Must I forego all these in hand, to live upon I know not what, and I know not who?" And so he took his leave of Christ (see Matthew 19:16–22). And the apostle said, "Demas hath forsaken me, having loved this present world" (2 Timothy 4:10). Their comforts, their enjoyments, their outward possessions, and their outward peace will be more to them than all that they ever thought of Christ, if they are not really interested in Him.

But now, as for the man who has given himself to Christ, his heart is so engaged, and he has tasted so much sweetness in Christ Jesus, that, whatever it costs him, Christ and he will never part. Though he is stripped naked for Christ, yet he will have Him. Though he dies for Christ, yet he will not give up his interest in Him.

Now, examine yourselves by the strong endearments of your hearts unto Christ. When there is an opposing interest that seems to come between you and Christ, do your affections then divide, and do you then deliver up Christ and give up your share in Him? By a close examination of your hearts under this heading, you may come to some knowledge of your present state as to your interest.

SIGN 15. The man who has an interest in Christ prefers the glory of Christ's interest before his own private advantage.

If you are indeed joined unto the Lord, then the interest of Christ's glory is a swaying interest in your hearts; it is a ruling, captivating interest that binds and engages you to the glory of it, so that the believer will prefer Christ's glory before anything of his own. His life will be under a peculiar dedication to advance and promote the glory of Christ Jesus, and he will be always designing to exalt Christ in his heart, to exalt Him in his house, and to exalt Him whatever he has to do and with whomever he has to do. He will exalt Christ though it is at the expense of his own name and of his own interest. He will deny his own name for Christ, and will believe for the advancing of the glory of the interest of his Lord. "To me to live is Christ, and to die is gain" (Philippians 1:21). The apostle sums up all in this: "Christ is my all; if I live, I desire not to live for myself, but for Christ; and if I die, I desire to die for Christ, so that His interest, and the glory of His interest, may be exalted by me both while I live and when I die."

Now, Christians, examine yourselves by this. What sway does the glory of Christ bear in your hearts? If you cannot deny yourselves for Christ, if your own names are more to you than His name, if your own honor is more to you than His honor, and if your own interest is more to you than His interest, it is a very ill sign that things are not right in your hearts. But if the interest of Christ is your ruling, swaying interest, if your design is to advance the glory of Christ, whatever becomes of yourselves, whatever becomes of your interests, and whatever you suffer in the way; if you say, "Oh, that Christ might be magnified! And, oh, that Christ might be glorified!"; if His glory is uppermost in your hearts, and is the only interest that you would prefer—it is a sign that you indeed have an interest in Christ, for otherwise your hearts would never be so concerned about His interest, and about the glory of His interest.

And to help and direct you a little further, consider these next few things.

In searching your own hearts for an evidence of interest, if you can in truth find these things that we have laid down, though not in high degrees and measures, you may be comforted. Many persons wrong their case, and so darken themselves thereupon, by looking more unto the height of those things that are notes of evidence than unto the truth of them. Now, examine yourselves, I say, by the truth of these things; though you cannot yet find that you have overcome temptation, that you have gotten a holy triumph over temptation, yet if you can find that, under all contrary inclinations and drawings, the habitual frame and inclination of your heart is secured for Christ, you may be comforted. Though you cannot find that you are able to do much towards the repairing of the glory of Christ in your place, yet if you have a heart that is deeply affected with the dishonor that is done to Christ because He is dishonored thereby, you may be comforted.

Though, Christians, you can find in your searches but very little of Christ in your hearts, yet if your souls pursue restlessly after Christ in all your seeking Him, so that you must attain to some real knowledge of Him or you cannot be satisfied, this seeking heart and restless spirit after Christ is a note of evidence to you. And though you cannot live up to Christ as you would, yet if your preparations and reformations are heart preparations and heart reformations, this may be a matter of comfort to you, and so you may go on to all the other particulars that I have given you. Look more to the truth of your evidences than to the height and degree of them, if you would come by them to a right understanding of your present state.

If upon a search you can find but some of those things that have been given you as evidential of an interest, you may be comforted though, for the present, you cannot speak of them all with experiential certainty. The Lord speaks unto one soul by one word and unto another soul by another word, and we do not know what particular word the Lord will make use of, nor what particular of all these the Lord has singled out, and made of use, advantage, or comfort to any of you. But if the Spirit of the Lord has singled out any one of them and given you a hint of interest thereupon, you have cause to rejoice in the Lord; and if the Lord has given you but the least hint of His love, and the least intimation (by any word of grace) of your interest, let not this be looked upon as a small thing. Take heed of refusing the consolations of the Lord when they are offered to you; remember him of whom it is said, "My soul refused to be comforted" (Psalm 77:2).

Know that full assurance and clear evidence of interest are gradually brought into the heart. As the light of grace comes in gradually, so also does the light of comfort, which is a light unto your souls to discern Christ, and to take comfort in Him. Now the Lord, it may be, at first lets in a little light, as it were, through the crevices; do not disregard this. This is how the Lord works. He gives a little light at one time, as it were, that puts the soul between hope and fear; and by and by He comes in with a little more light, and then with a little

more light, and so gradually He carries the believer until He has led him to a clear evidence and given him a
full assurance of interest. So if you have only the day-
star in your hearts, do not despise it; if you have just the
beginnings of the light of consolation, do not judge
this to be small. Though, compared to what some enjoy, it is but small, yet let it not be small in your apprehension; but know that the light of interest gradually
comes in and increases. I may liken the light of interest
to the prophet's cloud, which was at first but like a
man's hand, and it was a great way off; there was some
hope of rain upon it, but they did not know what would
come of it; but this was the beginning of a cloud that
brought an abundance of rain (see 1 Kings 18:44–45).

So, Christian, you have a little light glimmering in
your heart that sets you, it may be, between hope and
fear. Well, do not let this be small to you, for though for
the present you cannot come to a full assurance, yet you
do not know what this will come to. You do not know
what a growing light this is, and how much it may increase in your heart.

Now, unto those who have as yet but a little light in
their souls and some small hopes, through grace, of an
interest—those who dare not positively conclude but
dare not absolutely deny, that they have an interest;
those who do not have that full assurance which some
have, neither are they left wholly in the dark—unto
these souls I would speak something by way of encouragement and something by way of direction.

First, I speak by way of encouragement to those who
have a little hope through grace, some small glimmer-
ings of their interest, and some buddings of their evi-

dence, though they are not yet fully blown. Let such consider:

1. If you have anything that is a note of evidence, or gives you hope through grace (I mean, anything that is in truth), know that though it is ever so small, yet your interest in Christ is as great as his is who dwells in the height of assurance. My friends, your interest in Christ is not the less because your evidence of interest is very small; but your little evidence that is in truth, or this little word of grace that the Spirit has spoken that gives you some hopes about your condition, gives you as full an interest in Christ as he has who has the highest measures of assurance in this world. The young child who can but run to his father and cry, "Father, father," has as full an interest in and relation to his father as the grown child who, in understanding and judgment, is able to reflect upon and improve the relationship. And so it is with your soul in your union with Christ. Though you can but look up unto the Lord, and cry unto Him to help you; though you can but cry, "Father"; though you are not able to improve your interest as some others can, yet if, upon the least hint of grace from the Spirit, you are able to cry, "Father," your interest is as good and as great as his who is able to rejoice in Christ in full evidence. Christ is yours, and you are sons; you are heirs as well as others, and you have the same Spirit and the same Fountain of grace to go to under the smallness of the evidence of your interest.

2. You are under the same preserving, maintaining care as those who dwell upon the top of assurance. Jesus Christ does not take any less care of you because your interest is very dark and cloudy for the present, but His care over you is the same. He is always opening His

watchful eye upon you, and He is always doing for you, always defending you. Hear what He says: "He shall feed His flock like a shepherd. He shall gather the lambs with His arm, and carry them in His bosom, and shall gently lead those that are with young" (Isaiah 40:11). Alas, they are scarcely able to believe that they are lambs in the flock of Christ; they would hope so, and they dare not wholly deny it, but that Christ has a part in them, and has a hold on them, they scarcely venture to say. Nevertheless, they are under as much care as any. He will carry them in His arms. He will gently lead those who are with young. Christ Jesus, in one single act, equally respects all those who have an interest in Him, be their evidence of interest more or less, clearer or more clouded.

3. The extent to which Christ carries out the union is not proportioned unto, but far exceeds our apprehensions of Him in the union. Christ does not say, "I will be unto you as you are unto Me; as you do, so will I do; as you are, so will I be; and according to your apprehensions, so will I be unto you." But He does exceedingly abundantly for us above our faith and above our hope. It may be that we can only say unto Him, "Lord, help." Even though we are so weak, He will not do less, but He will prosecute and manage His interest in your souls, though your apprehensions of Him may be very small. You have a very full and satisfying Scripture for this: "Now unto Him that is able to do exceeding abundantly above all that we ask or think, according to the power that worketh in us" (Ephesians 3:20). Jesus Christ's actings towards us and His dealings with us are not proportioned to our apprehensions of Him, nor according to our faith and hope, nor according to our

prayer. Rather the apostle says, He is "able to do exceeding abundantly above all that we are able to ask or think," and that "according to the power that worketh in us." So that, though you cannot at all times exercise faith in that power, yet that power is working; and though your apprehensions are very small, yet the mercies of Christ are very great. It is in heaven that we shall know as we are known; we are fully known here, but we know only in part.

4. All your weaknesses and provocations will be covered and forgiven by the Lord Jesus, in the strength of the love of His relation to you or interest in you. The believer who is related to Christ is not able, in a clear gospel way, to live up to his standing in Christ Jesus, but oftentimes walks very dishonorably unto his interest and very unbecomingly to his hopes of evidence. Well, soul, though it is thus, the Lord Jesus Christ will display such love on His part as shall cover and forgive all. The father will not disinherit his child because he provokes him, and because he grieves him by many foolish and unchildlike acts; but the father, in his love for the relation, will forgive the child. The husband will not divorce his wife because he finds failings in her ways, but the love of the relation binds and influences him to cover all her weaknesses, and continue his kindness to her. If we have a member that is full of pain, puts us to a great deal of smart, and puts us much out of order, we do not immediately cut off this member, but we bear with the pain and smart, remembering that it is a member of the body.

Now, thus it is, my friends, between the Lord Jesus Christ and you. Though weaknesses are discovered in your ways, yet He will remember that you have an interest in Him; and though He meets with provocations from you, yet He will remember that you are His children, and what you are in relation, and that will engage Him to cover and forgive all. I do not say this to give any a liberty to indulge themselves (I hope none of you will so abuse discoveries of grace. I am sure an honest heart will not), but only if some of you are tempted to become terrified. Know that though Jesus Christ will not proceed, in the utmost of His displeasure against you to give you a bill of divorce, though there are rebukes and frowns as bitter as death that the soul may receive from Christ upon His high provocations. Though we do not instantly cut off a member that is full of pain, yet we may see cause to send for the surgeon to make an incision. And so verily will Jesus Christ be forced to do in your hearts who give yourselves such an allowance. "If his children forsake My law, and walk not in My judgments; if they break My statutes, and keep not My commandments; then will I visit their transgression with the rod, and their iniquity with stripes. Neverthe-less My loving-kindness will I not utterly take from him, nor suffer My faithfulness to fail" (Psalm 89:30–33).

5. Know that your interest in Christ cannot be dissolved even though the evidence of your interest may be lost. Christian, it may be that the Lord has singled out some word that He has made use of by His Spirit to give you some hope about your interest in and relation to Christ. I would hope that all has not been spoken to you in vain, but if the Lord has given you some hint by His word of your interest, possibly within a little while all this will be lost again, and you may be as much in the dark as you ever were since you came to Christ.

Well, Christ will not disown you, but will rather hold you up so that you shall never be left to disown Him. Your interest in Christ Jesus is still sure. Though light is coming and going in your soul, and your evidence is sometimes coming and sometimes going, yet know that your interest is firm and inviolable.

6. Your present interest in and relation unto Christ in a state of grace is a certain and infallible pledge of your future possession of Christ in glory. Christian, you have a little hope through grace. Oh, make much of it, for you do not know what is in it. There is not only matter of consolation in it, but it contains a pledge of heaven, and of your full possession of the Lord Jesus Christ in glory forever. Therefore Christ said, "He that believeth on Me hath everlasting life" (John 6:47). It is believing that gives the interest whereby the soul is united to Christ. As a result of the union he has everlasting life. His union is the pledge of it. He is reserved for eternal life, and he is going on to perfection to enjoy eternal life. The Lord is, in and by grace, fitting him for a glorious enjoyment of Himself forever. Now, these things are for your comfort in your present condition, while the light of evidence is but glimmering in your heart.

Some few things, briefly, I shall now give you by way of direction.

1. Have you the least intimation of the Lord's love for you, and of your standing in His love? Be thankful for these small appearances of light in your souls. I say, be thankful, Christians. There is a great deal in a little word of evidence, or in a small word of hope. Therefore, take every hint that the Lord gives, wear it with

thankfulness, and bless His name for it, for that is the way to have it increased.

2. Rejoice and triumph in the Lord upon the present evidence that you have, living up to it. I say, live up to the light that you have in a holy joy and rejoicing in Christ Jesus; get into the prophet's spirit, and into his frame as in our text, so as to joy in the Lord and rejoice in the God of your salvation. And learn, Christian, to live up unto a small measure of assurance, for that is the way to have a greater one.

3. Acknowledge that all sense of interest is given forth in a way of grace. I say, acknowledge that not only the grace of your union, but also the light and comfort of your union are dispensed in a way of free grace. The Lord is pleased to give out all manifestations of interest in Christ in a way of grace. "Judas saith unto Him, not Iscariot, 'Lord, how is it that Thou wilt manifest Thyself unto us, and not unto the world' "? (John 14:22). He must have spoken this upon a reflection, or else he could not speak with such confidence. "Lord, that Thou hast manifested Thyself to us, and not to others"—this is to be acknowledged as a gift of free grace.

4. Seek for a full enjoyment of the Lord Jesus. Have you a little light of your interest? Then come unto Christ from that little that you have, seeking for more. Christians, though you have but a little light for the present, and are weak in assurance for the present, yet there is a full measure of assurance to be given out. There is not only the believer's comfort upon reflection, by the light of the Lord through His own grace that is wrought, but the immediate testimony of the Spirit is ready to be given out, which is not a witness by way of argumentation, but a witness and evidence by

and in the immediateness of His own presence in the heart of the believer. So "the Spirit itself beareth witness with our spirit that we are the children of God" (Romans 8:16). He bears witness in some immediate act in the soul. It is a clear, undeniable, soul-satisfying, divine testimony that the Spirit gives in the soul, resolving all the believer's doubts and making plain to him his whole interest, settling him in the full enjoyment of the Lord Jesus, and enabling him to act upon it.

5. Venture upon Christ and live upon Christ. Have you a little evidence of your interest for the present? Then, Christian, improve this little unto the comforting of your soul in Christ in all straits, and unto a living upon Him in all the necessities of your present condition. Jesus is yours, and you have an interest in Him; the Lord has given you some little hope of this. Make use of this hope through grace, Christian. Upon all occasions you should run out unto the Lord Jesus, have recourse to Him, and venture upon Him. You should glory in Him, live upon His fullness, and rely upon His power and faithfulness. Jesus, who is so full, is your Jesus. Jesus, who is so free, is your Jesus. Jesus, who is so faithful, is your Jesus. You have some sight of this, and some hope of this through grace. The Lord now expects that you should come and live upon Him in all conditions, and comfort your souls in Him in all disconsolations. When you are weak, when you are tempted, when you are tried, and when you meet with discouragements from without, then retire to the Lord Jesus and exercise faith in Him.

Chapter 6

*Some Considerations to Encourage Believers
to Rejoice in the Lord Jesus Christ*

I shall now proceed to help and direct those souls that are able to reflect upon their own interest and standing in Christ, so that they may live upon Christ and glory in Him in all conditions, and under all changes of providence; so that, though they have no one else and have nothing else in this world but the Lord Jesus Christ to live upon, their hearts may be full of joy and comfort. But before speaking of this I shall put before you certain considerations, with the hope that in so doing I may make clearer to you that which I propose to speak about, and likewise encourage your hearts to live upon and glory in Christ when you have nothing else to rejoice in.

CONSIDERATION 1. All the comforts of an outward condition are great uncertainties, and are continued at the sovereign pleasure of the great Disposer of heaven.

The Lord has not made us unchangeable in the enjoyments and comforts of an outward state, but He reserves a sovereign power in His own hand to take back from us what at time He was pleased to bestow. All the comforts of an outward condition are changeable, and we are exposed to a variety of changes of condition in this world. All our outward comforts are exposed to spoilage, and the very foundation of our joy in this world is weak. He who has, by his own apprehension, a mountain that stands strong, one that he thinks can never be moved, is exposed to the sovereign alterations of the great Ruler of heaven, so that he may have his mountain overturned in a moment; and he who is lifted up on high, and seems to himself to be so advanced that he shall never fall, the Lord can suddenly, as He did with Job, lay him in the dust.

We are full one day, and the Lord may empty us before the next; we are rich today, and we may be poor before tomorrow; we are comforted today on every side, and we may be left naked, destitute, and broken before tomorrow. Our possessions can be lost or expended; all lands and inheritances can be sold or mortgaged. Like uncertain riches, they make wings for themselves and fly away; they have the wings of fire, or the wings of thieves, or the wings of this or that providence to fly away with. The Lord suffers one man to run away with so much of such a man's estate, and suffers another to run away with another part of it, so that those who were rich are soon made poor. And as for your relations that you at present take comfort in, now they are and anon they are not. Parents, children, friends, comforters, counselers, all die away from us; we see them, and then we know them no more forever.

Any of you who are here today may one day sit down and weep over your broken pitchers, and say, "Once I had this, and once I had that, but now I have nothing. Once I was full, but now I am empty; once I was lifted up on high, but now I am brought down very low; once I was a lender, but now I am a borrower. Once I had the most comfortable relationships; none was happier than I in a tender father, in a loving spouse, in a desirable child, in a faithful friend. But now it is quite otherwise; they are all like Jonah's gourd that grew up and withered all of a sudden." This you may see in the verse before our text; the fig tree blossoms not, the fruit of the vine and the labor of the olive fail, the fields yield no meat, the flocks are cut off from the fold, and there is no herd in the stall. The Lord has given us but a weak tenure to all these outward enjoyments, and He maintains a sovereignty over every comfort that He is pleased to bestow upon us, so that we may view all that we have in this world as great uncertainties, and we must daily depend on the allowance of the great Disposer of heaven, who will sometimes give and will sometimes take what He has given.

CONSIDERATION 2. The Lord Jesus Christ is and has whatever the Scripture has said, and much more than we are able to conceive of Him in our largest and utmost apprehensions.

He is and He has, according unto all Old Testament prophecies and predictions, in the utmost exposition that can be made of them and to the largest extent; and He is and He has according to the utmost word of the revelation that is made of Him in the New Testament. And you are not able to conceive or apprehend what He is and what He has in considering the Scripture expressions that are used to set Him forth unto you. You cannot measure Christ by your thoughts and imaginations; but when you have conceived all that you can, Christ is more, and Christ has more, than you are able to apprehend of Him. The Scripture tells us that the Lord Jesus Christ has a fullness of grace in Him. Now, you are not able to apprehend what this fullness of grace is; it is an infinite fullness, and you are not able to comprehend it in your finite thoughts, however comprehensive they are.

The gospel tells you of how Christ's heart goes out unto sinners, but you are not able to apprehend or measure the love of Christ's heart for poor sinners; for when you have conceived ever so much of His love, there is more still than you are able to grasp. The Scripture tells you of the great power that is in Christ. Conceive ever so much of this power, what it is that He is able to do for you in a time of trial, and how wonderfully He is able to work, but there is yet a greater extent in the power of Christ than your apprehensions can reach. The gospel tells you of an all-fullness, or an "all-ness," that is in the Lord Jesus Christ. Sum up all that you can think of, and all that the Scripture can help you to conceive of, to add unto this "all-ness" of Christ, and yet, behold, you are not able to tell what His all is.

You may soon tell what your all is, or you may tell what another's all is, what a great man's all is, what a prince's all is, or what a kingdom's all is; but you cannot tell what Christ's all is. For when you have thought and conceived, when you have dived and reached until you are weary, still the grace, the power, the love, and the fullness of the Lord Jesus are above your reach, and there is more than ever entered into your hearts to conceive of Him. Isaiah 55:8–9: " 'For My thoughts are not your thoughts, neither are your ways My ways,' saith the Lord. 'For as the heavens are higher than the earth, so are My ways higher than your ways, and My thoughts than your thoughts.' " See how the Lord teaches us that He is advanced above all our imaginations of Him. Now, the thoughts of Christ's heart are always towards us, and always proportioned unto the fullness that He has received. He says, "My thoughts are not like your thoughts. You thought that I could relieve only in such a case, or that I could help only in such a trial; you thought I could only do this and no more. But you are mistaken; there is as great a distance between My thoughts and your thoughts as there is between heaven and earth." So the fullness of Christ Jesus is a most glorious and blessed fullness, enough for all your soul's relief and some to spare.

CONSIDERATION 3. Christ's fullness of grace is always subjectively and objectively the same.

First, it is always subjectively the same. Christ's spring is not a rising and a falling spring, but the waters of it are always of the same depth; the waters of this fountain do not admit of an ebb and of a flow, but they are always at one and the same height. Christ does not have a more and a less. His fullness will not admit of an augmentation and a diminution, but, notwithstanding all the overflowings of the fountain, still it is a fountain-fullness; notwithstanding all the streams that have run from it, still it is as full as ever; notwithstanding all the thousands of souls whom Jesus has relieved and empty hearts that Jesus has filled, still He is as full of grace as ever, as full of mercy as ever. There is no less in this fountain, as it is subjectively considered, after all that He has given and dispensed; but He is as rich in grace, and there is as great a plenty in Him, as when He first opened His fountain unto sinners. "For it pleased the Father that in Him should all fullness dwell" (Colossians 1:19). There it always abides, the same fullness without change, the same fullness without diminution. That fullness which God placed in His Son abides in the glory of its utmost height. "Jesus Christ the same yesterday, today, and forever" (Hebrews 13:8). This is said of your Jesus. His fullness was a great fullness at first, but He is the same today. Spend, Christians, what you will, and draw out of the fountain what you can, it will be as full tomorrow as it is today. He is the same yesterday, today, and forever.

Second, Christ's fullness is always objectively the same for all those who possess it. The soul that has an interest in Jesus once has an interest in Him forever. And the soul that is once admitted unto the fountain of Christ Jesus shall never be barred again. You do not have a coming and a going interest, an interest that exists today and may be taken away tomorrow. Your outward comforts are losable, and your outward blessings are spendable. God may give you much today, and you may have nothing of all that much tomorrow. But it is not so here: you are not interested in Christ today and uninterested in Him tomorrow; rather once interested, forever interested. We cannot be gracious now and graceless by and by, but our interest in the grace of Christ is an everlasting interest; and you have the immutable fullness of the Lord Jesus ever to go unto, whatever your strait is, once an interest in Him is given to you. The Lord does not give you a part in Himself and then take away that part, but Christ, once yours, is forever yours. And none shall ever be able to take from you or deprive you of your Fountain-fullness. Once you have Christ to go to, you always have Christ to go to, and once you discern your interest in Christ upon good and Scriptural grounds, you may always glory in the Lord, whom you have once gained an interest in.

CONSIDERATION 4. All saints have the same Lord Jesus to live upon, and the same fullness of Christ in all its dimensions to go to.

The Lord has not given one believer a greater proprietorship in Himself than He has given another; neither has one a fuller way prepared for him to go to Christ than another has. The same Jesus that Abraham had to do with, and upon whom he lived, is in common for every son and daughter of Abraham; and the same fullness of Jesus that Abraham had, you have in all its dimensions. The Lord did not open a fountain unto Abraham and only a stream unto you. On the contrary, if you are a son or daughter of Abraham, you have the same great ocean to go unto in all its fullness that Abraham had; you have the same merits to plead that Abraham had; you have the same blood to cleanse you that any other believer has; and you have the same great and precious promises to apply that any other believer has. One believer cannot lay a challenge upon this promise and say, "It is mine, and not yours." Rather, it is yours as well as mine. The same Fountain in all its dimensions is available in all your trials as it is to another believer. Therefore, if you do not have that strength, if you do not have that grace, if you do not have those riches, if you do not have that fullness which another believer has, you must blame yourselves and not Christ; for He offers Himself alike unto all, and reveals and holds forth His fountain alike unto all.

CONSIDERATION 5. There is a vast disproportion between your earthly losses and your gains and enjoyments in Christ.

Your losses in this world are but shadows and not substance; there is an emptiness in the fullest outward condition, considered as an outward condition, and a bitterness in the sweetest outward enjoyment; the losses that you may meet with in this world are only such as reach and concern a physical life. But there is more in a little of Christ Jesus than there is in a great deal of the world, nay, in all wordly enjoyments. So whatever the loss is that you meet with in the world, a little of Christ Jesus will make it up. The least gift of Christ's right hand far exceeds all the gifts of His left hand, and one draught of the water of the upper springs is more than all the waters in the nether springs. So though you meet with sore losses, great blows, and sufferings in the outward man, yet know that a little of Christ will fill up your soul so that there will be no want, whatever you have lost. It may be, Christian, that the things you have lost would have been enjoyed to your disadvantage if they had still been kept in your hand; it may be that they would had led to the loss or the hurt of the possessor. But now Jesus Christ is always enjoyed to your advantage, and Christ Jesus is such an advantage as will answer all losing disadvantages. Hence, Christian, do not be overly dejected at the passing away of worldly things, when there is still enough in Christ to make up the loss that you have sustained.

CONSIDERATION 6. The joy that is drawn from Christ does not depend upon sensible things, but lives in the soul when all outward comforts are gone.

You may, as to the world, be an undone man, broken in your outward estate, and yet your joy none can take from you. Whatsoever you have in this world, if you do not have Christ with it, you have no ground of joy.

But Christ is always a ground of joy, whether these other things are absent or present; material things, however, are never so without Christ. Consider the Apostle Paul; he had an interest in Christ, and he gloried in his interest when he had nothing else. "We have peace with God, through our Lord Jesus Christ . . . and rejoice in hope of the glory of God. And, therefore, we glory in tribulation" (Romans 5:1–3). We are spoiled in our goods; we are sorely broken and left sorrowful, desolate, and forsaken as to outward supports and supporters. Yet, said Paul, in the midst of all, "we glory in tribulation." Or, if you will, according unto another Scripture, we are "as sorrowful" and "as poor, yet we make many rich" (2 Corinthians 6:10). We have grace, and an abundance of grace in Christ Jesus, and we are in no want.

Paul and Silas were in prison, and in the stocks, and yet, behold, at midnight they broke out singing praises unto God (Acts 16:25). Their hearts were full of joy when they had nothing of the world in their hands. And thus behaved the prophet in our text; there came a famine upon all his outward comforts, and, behold, he had nothing to live upon, and yet he said, "I will rejoice in the Lord." We have all in Him when we have nothing outside of Him. Joy that is drawn from Christ shall abide in the soul when all visible creature supports shall fail. Though his entertainment in the world is very mean, his outward burdens very great, and his poverty very pressing upon his outward man, yet the soul that has an interest in Christ will joy, notwithstanding all this.

CONSIDERATION 7. The Lord Jesus Christ, in His gospel-fullness of grace, is under an indispensable obligation to dispense that grace of which, as the great officer of heaven, He has received the charge.

The fullness of Christ Jesus is a common fullness; it is a fullness for all believers. And Jesus Christ does not live and spend upon the fullness of grace that He has received, but He reveals it to the saints so that they may have it to live upon. He lies under indispensable obligations to dispense it to those who come to Him. Jesus Christ will not bar any soul that comes unto Him for spiritual relief. He is engaged in faithfulness to His Father to relieve those who come, and He must deny His office (which He can never do) if He does not do it; for the Father has entrusted Him with grace so that He might dispense it. And He has given Him this fullness so that He might communicate of it to those who are in want. "Thou hast ascended on high. Thou hast led captivity captive. Thou hast received gifts for men" (Psalm 68:18). Jesus Christ has received great gifts from His Father. He has received grace gifts and office gifts, and He has received personal gifts—and all these gifts that He has received are for men. "All things are yours, whether Paul, or Apollos, or Cephas, or the world . . . or things present or things to come; all are yours" (1 Corinthians 3:21–22).

All that Christ has received from His Father, or is ordained to dispense, He must dispense and He will dispense. "The Spirit of the Lord God is upon Me, because the Lord hath anointed Me to preach good tidings unto the meek. He hath sent Me to bind up the broken-hearted, to proclaim liberty to the captives, and the opening of the prison to them that are bound" (Isaiah 61:1–2). "There is a poor soul," Christ says, "that I must deliver; there is a wounded heart that I must heal; there is a bruised reed that I must bind up, and there is one weak in grace whom I must strengthen." And why must He do it? "Why, He says, "I am anointed to do this." The Father has commissioned Him to do this. He has ordained Him hereunto, and Christ would have to deny His ordination, and refuse the office that He is to act in, should He refuse a poor soul and not give liberally to those who come to Him. "Labor not for the meat which perisheth, but for that meat which endureth unto everlasting life, which the Son of man shall give unto you; for Him hath God the Father sealed" (John 6:27). In these expressions are discovered the great blessings of the gospel that are dispensable by the hands of Christ.

Now, go unto Christ if you are hungry; if you are thirsty, go unto Christ Jesus; if you are naked or empty, go unto Christ Jesus. "Why, will He bless such a one as I am? Will He look upon such a one as I am?" you ask. "Yes," says the Father, "go, and you shall succeed. My Son shall give these things to you, for I have sealed Him." Or you may consider these words as spoken by Christ, and as the indispensable obligation that lies upon the Son from the charge that He has received, a charge for all that grace which the Father has designed should be dispensed. Do not question, therefore, the Lord Jesus Christ, but let your applications to Him be frequent. He will be faithful unto His office.

CONSIDERATION 8. There is an exceeding tenderness in the heart of Christ unto distressed sinners, according to all the designs of His office.

There is a very great willingness and forwardness in the Lord Jesus Christ to be dealing out His grace unto those for whom grace was designed, or to whom grace is to be dispensed. There is an inexpressible desire in the soul of Christ Jesus to be dealing out the grace that He has received the charge of. All the work to which He has been anointed by the Father in His offices as Prophet, Priest, and King is most desirable work to Christ, though ever so hard. Therefore, when He speaks concerning His death, He says, "I have a baptism to be baptized with; and how am I straitened till it be accomplished!" (Luke 12:50). But now we may conceive that there is a much greater desire in the heart of Christ to dispense the grace of His death. "Thou art My Lord. My goodness extendeth not to Thee, but to the saints that are in the earth, and to the excellent, in whom is all My delight" (Psalm 16:2–3). "My delight," says Christ, "is with the saints, to be relieving the saints, to be comforting the saints, and to be blessing and strengthening the saints." The heart of Christ takes great delight in this. "My delight is with them as to all My goodness, as to all my kindness, as to all the gifts of grace that I have received, and as to all My fountain-fullness. It does not extend to Me, but it is for the saints; and My delight is with the saints, on the consideration of the grace that I have to dispense to them."

Hence, Jesus Christ is touched with us (see Hebrews 4:15). He has a feeling for our infirmities—not a feeling in a way of passion and suffering, but a feeling in a way of compassion and tenderness. As the mother has a feeling for the pain, sickness, and weariness of the child, through the sympathy of her spirit and the yearnings of her heart over it, so the Lord Jesus Christ stands with a yearning heart over His children, for He is touched with the feeling of our infirmities. You cannot have a weight upon your spirit but in compassion and tenderness Jesus Christ feels it; and you do not have a burden in any respect but Jesus Christ feels it. Such are the compassions of His spirit toward you in all the concerns of His office. It may be that you are ready to say, in a great strait or under a sore trial, "Oh, that such a friend knew how it is with me! Oh, that my father were here, or that such a relation were here! If they only knew how it is with me!" Why, soul, Jesus Christ knows, and He feels the weight of your troubles, and sympathizes with you under all your sorrows. "We have not a High Priest which cannot be touched with the feeling of our infirmities" (Hebrews 4:15). Now, this tenderness of spirit, this sympathy of Christ, influences His hand unto a liberal and free discharge of His office, so that whatever are your losses in this world, and however your outward condition is broken, you may go to the Lord Jesus, for you see He is such a one as you may take comfort in.

CONSIDERATION 9. Faith is the great instrumental means that receives from Christ and that establishes the soul in Christ.

All our blessings are lodged in the Lord Jesus Christ, and there they meet as in a fountain. Now, faith is the drawing grace that draws out of this Fountain for the soul's supply. The Father has placed all in Christ, and faith is the receiving grace that takes all out of the hand of Jesus Christ that He offers to the soul. By faith we are united to Christ, and by faith we receive from Christ upon the union. As the pipe that is laid to the mouth of the fountain receives and conveys water into your house, so faith receives from the Lord Jesus Christ and conveys it into your souls. Faith is the great conduit by which Jesus Christ sends down His grace into

our hearts. Faith that deals with Christ in all His royalties of grace—takes life from Him, takes comfort from
Him, takes peace from Him and joy from Him, and
whatsoever the soul stands in need of—is the life-grace
that feeds your souls, that keeps you living and thriving,
and that makes you strong in the Lord. We are said,
therefore, to stand by faith. "Because of unbelief they
were broken off, and thou standest by faith" (Romans
11:20). Faith is a confirming grace; it builds the soul
upon and roots the soul in the Lord Jesus Christ, and
receives strengthening, confirming, and assisting
grace from Christ, according to the soul's necessity.
Hence, Christians, if you would be strong in the Lord,
you must get your faith strengthened more and more.

CONSIDERATION 10. The Lord Christ, in dispensing mercy, has great respect for the glory of His office-
fullness and office-faithfulness.

The Lord Christ, in the communications of grace,
not only has a respect unto your necessity, but also to
His own glory; and He will dispense in such a way, and
at such a season and under such circumstances, as
shall do the most for the glory of His office-fullness
and office-faithfulness. The Lord Jesus Christ, therefore, comes in such a way and at such a time as shall
most of all publish His glory unto those to whom He
comes, and before whom He comes.

When a person has run into emptiness and spent
all, then Jesus Christ opens His fountain-fullness. In
the weakness of the creature Jesus Christ displays His
all-sufficiency, and in the uncertainty of the creature
Jesus Christ glorifies His constancy. In the darkness of
an outward condition the Lord Jesus Christ causes His
morning star to arise and shine from on high, and that

gives light to our feet when we know not how to direct our own paths. When we have lost all here below, and all our comforts have failed us and forsaken us, then Jesus Christ appears as a Friend who stands up in a time of adversity, so that neither troubles nor crosses nor trials nor temptations shall separate us from Him. And He chooses this most dismal state to come in so that He might glorify His office-fullness and His office-faithfulness. He will glorify His office-fullness to let us know that it is a never-failing fullness; it is a fullness that is always running over, that is not dry when streams are dry, but that can fill streams at any time, when they are ever so dry and empty. And then He comes that He may glorify His office-faithfulness, to appear as one who never forgets His people, one who can bear all the concerns of His people upon His heart.

So 2 Corinthians 1:9 says, "But we had the sentence of death in ourselves." Thus the Lord Jesus Christ comes, and reveals Himself when the sentence of death is upon our outward mercies and upon all our outward supporters; when they are fading, dying, and falling down under us, then the Lord Jesus Christ appears as our God. We have the sentence of death in ourselves so that we might trust in the living God. The Lord will appear in such a way that His appearance shall be unto the glory of His own name in the office that He is placed in by the Father. And, therefore, consider what titles Jesus Christ has put upon Himself. "The Lord also will be a refuge for the oppressed, a refuge in times of trouble" (Psalm 9:9). To a poor distressed soul that has nowhere to go, that is driven off from all his former holds, and that has all his other wells of consolation dried up, Jesus will be a refuge to such a one, especially in the time of trouble. "The poor committeth himself unto Thee; Thou art the Helper of the fatherless" (Psalm 10:14). "A Father of the fatherless, and a Judge of the widows, is God in His holy habitation" (Psalm 68:5).

"Why," says the soul, "now all is gone; my father is gone, my husband is gone, my friends who used to comfort me have left me, and I am now a miserable creature."

"No," says Christ, "this is My time to appear, to show Myself to be a Father to the fatherless and a Judge of the widow." Isaiah 25:4: "Thou hast been a refuge from the storm, a shadow from the heat, when the blast of the terrible ones is as a storm against the wall."

Why, Christian, do not fear an outward distress then; do not fear a low condition; do not fear a trying providence—because Jesus Christ then makes it His time to reveal His all to you. He will then take that time to reveal a fountain to you that can never be exhausted, for He is a refuge to the poor and needy. And these considerations should be prevailing upon your spirits to gather your eyes from beholding other objects, and to place them upon the Lord Jesus Christ, where there is a sufficient ground of joy for us, whatever our condition is.

CONSIDERATION 11. To believe in the Lord Jesus Christ without the least encouragement of sense is the most noble exercise of faith, and that which most pleases the Lord.

To believe in the Lord Jesus Christ when He is breaking you, when He is frowning upon you, and when you have nothing else to live upon—this is the most noble exercise of faith in this life. To believe on the Lord Jesus when your table is spread and when your borders are enlarged is no great difficulty. But now, to live by faith upon Christ when there is no encouragement from the world is the most noble exercise of faith.

"What?" says sense, "live by faith upon Christ when He has impoverished me and emptied me of all worldly enjoyments?" Yes, now is the time to exercise faith, and this is the most noble exercise of faith, and that which most of all pleases the Lord.

Such an exercise of faith as this was found in Job. When the Lord had taken away his estate and his children, Job said, "Blessed be the name of the Lord" (Job 1:21). There was a great exercise of faith in those words. And such an exercise of faith was found in David in the case of Ziklag. He had a little place given him in the enemy's country where he might live alone, but he did not have it long before enemies came and smote the place of his habitation, took away his family and his goods, and left him nothing but ruins, so that when he returned he found nothing but emptiness and a heap of ashes (see 1 Samuel 30). What did David do then? He exercised faith and encouraged himself in the Lord his God. And this is the exercise of faith that the prophet speaks of in our text, and that to which he is exciting believers: "Although the fig tree shall not blossom, neither shall fruit be in the vines; the labor of the olive shall fail, and the fields shall yield no meat; the flock shall be cut off from the fold, and there shall be no herd in the stalls." What is here left? Here is nothing for sense to live upon. "Yet," he says, "I will rejoice in the Lord. I will joy in the God of my salvation."

Such a noble exercise of faith was found in the woman of Canaan, in the midst of all her discourage-

ments (see Matthew 15:22–28). She had discouragements from the disciples of Christ; they were not so
kind to her as they might have been. But that was not
all; she met with discouragements from the Lord Jesus
Christ Himself, unto whom she made her application.
He seemed to repulse her, and checked her forwardness; and yet she went over to the Lord Jesus and, in a
bold act, ventured upon Him alone.

Why, Christians, whatever your discouragements
from sense are, yet, in the face of all rebukes, to cast
yourselves upon the Lord Jesus and comfort your souls
in His all-sufficiency is the most noble act of faith that
you can put forth.

CONSIDERATION 12. The great improbabilities of
relief and succor after grace, whatever your case is, are
not to be compared to the improbabilities that your
souls were in before grace, and Christ Jesus then
helped you.

Christ came through all obstacles, and with ease removed them to do your souls good. Consider, you who
sit down with your hearts full of discouragement upon
the loss of something or upon the emptyings of providence, how unlikely and improbable your condition
was of finding help and succor before you believed in
Christ. You were then covered over with the shadow of
death; you were then in a hopeless condition. Who had
then any hope for you? When you were seen marching
in the fury of your spirits against the Lord, who would
have thought that there was hope in the Lord for you?
You were at the very brink of death, at the very brink of
hell. There was, as it were, but a hair's breadth between
you and hell; and who would have thought that you
should be recovered? Then the Lord Jesus broke

through all the improbabilities of your state to save you; and do you think that He cannot break through all the improbabilities of your present state to comfort you? He came leaping over greater mountains of opposition, discouragement, and impossibility (I mean, as to other help); I say, He came leaping over greater mountains of impossibility in His first dealings with you than there are for Him to come through in His later dealings with you. "The voice of my Beloved! Behold, He cometh leaping upon the mountains, skipping upon the hills" (Song of Solomon 2:8). These mountains and hills that lay between Christ and you were the improbabilities, or, I may call them, the impossibilities of your state, as to help and relief in a rational consideration and apprehension. Now, Jesus Christ leaped over this mountain and the other mountains that lay in His way, and He came unto your souls to do you good. And if Jesus Christ has done this, do you think that He will not do the lesser? When you were without grace, did He not bring grace into your souls? And do you think that He cannot comfort you now when you lack comfort? Do you think that He cannot bless you with the promised blessings of your present state when He has brought in the great fundamental blessings of your eternal state?

Christians, you should reason thus: "I was once ready to die, and the Lord Jesus came and saved me. I was in a soul-undone state, and Jesus Christ has set me up. He has He set up my soul, and can He not set up my body? Has He made up the great breach that was upon my spiritual condition, and can He not make up the breaches that are in my outward condition? Jesus Christ came and plucked me out of the fire when I was burning, and when the fire was so hot that none could take me out but Himself. He came and snatched me out of the paw of the lion and the bear, and no one besides Him could have rescued me." And do you think that He who came over all these impossibilities to save you cannot repair the breach in the loss of a relation, or a distress in your outward condition? The Lord who has done the greater thing can easily do the lesser one.

CONSIDERATION 13. To rejoice only in things seen and felt is to go no further than those may go who have no interest in Christ.

I pray you to consider this. To have your spirits borne up only by sensible supports is not to exceed those who are strangers to Jesus Christ, who do not have the interest in Jesus Christ that you have. If your spirits rise and fall only as the creature ebbs and flows, this is no more than a carnal man does. Is this living upon Christ? Is this to make Christ your joy, and the peace and comfort of your life? Christ said in another case, "If ye love them which love you, what reward have ye? Do not even the publicans the same?" (Matthew 5:46). The Christian is under peculiar and distinguishing blessings, and it is expected that he should peculiarly and distinguishingly live under the distinguishing blessings of his state. "Therefore take no thought, saying, 'What shall we eat?' or, 'What shall we drink?' or, 'Wherewithal shall we be clothed?' For after all these things do the Gentiles seek" (Matthew 6:31–32). It is typical of a Gentile to say, when his outward comforts are gone, "Oh, now I must die! Now there is no further help for me, I must now perish!" This is the language of a Gentile who has no interest in Jesus Christ. O you who have an interest in Jesus Christ, will you take up the language of a Gentile? Oh, no. Having a God to go to, you must live upon that God whom you have given yourselves up to. God expects your spiritual life to be conformed to the blessings that He has brought into your condition. Therefore, know that to rejoice only in things seen is to put yourselves in the same place with those who have no interest in Christ; and is this not to dishonor your interest, and to reflect ill upon the Lord of your interest, to live in joy when the creatures are about you, and to sit down discouraged when creature things are taken from you?

CONSIDERATION 14. Faith exercised upon the Lord Jesus will have a universal influence upon all other graces in your hearts.

Christians, do but once exercise faith upon the Lord Jesus Christ under a sinking, discouraging providence, and you will immediately find a strange alteration in your hearts. You will find those graces that are weak beginning to gather strength; and you will find those graces to arise, appear, and shine forth that you could scarcely discern before.

Faith exercised upon the Lord Jesus Christ will have a mighty influence upon your love, when the soul has gotten into Christ and can improve his interest in Christ. Oh, how will his soul be enlarged, and how his heart burn in love to Him who is the Lord of his interest and of his comforts! Faith exercised upon the Lord Jesus will have a mighty influence upon your hopes, so that your fears will be quenched. Faith exercised upon the Lord Jesus will have a mighty influence upon your patience, to strengthen and quicken it when a frowning providence comes that would chafe your spirits, put you beside yourselves, and drive you out of a Christian frame. Faith will raise up your patience and teach you to be quiet under the hand of the Lord. Faith exercised upon Christ will have an influence upon your joy; it will cause a mighty and wonderful rejoicing in your souls that you have such a full Jesus to live upon.

Faith exercised upon the Lord Jesus will have an influence upon your zeal, and will wonderfully excite you and stir you up unto all duties of serving and following the Lord. So, Christians, lay these considerations together, and you will see what great encouragement you have to glory in the Lord Jesus Christ, whatever your outward condition is. You will see the way of living by faith in Christ to be clear, and to be the only way that the Christian should walk in.

Chapter 7

Particular Directions as to Rejoicing in the Lord Jesus Christ in Every Condition

I shall now give you some particular directions as to how you may raise your faith, and your spirits in the exercise of faith, unto a glorying and rejoicing in the Lord Jesus Christ whatever your saddening, outward providences may be.

DIRECTION 1. If you would come to live upon Christ Jesus alone in the saddest providences of your state, then entertain and keep up low thoughts of the great things of this world.

Truly, Christians, you may think what you will, but while you have hearts that are magnifying and adoring the things of the world and the enjoyments of the world, and counting these as great things, you will never come scripturally to live upon the Lord Jesus. Your thoughts must be altered in and about the comforts of this life, and you must possess your hearts with the thought that these are the smallest comforts of your state, and that the blessings of this life are the least blessings that the Lord has given you. You must have very low thoughts of the world, and of the comforts of it, if you would come to live by faith in Christ Jesus alone. While you have vast thoughts of your earthly enjoyments, earthly comforts, and earthly conditions, and suppose your comforts to lie here, there, or anywhere

171

short of Christ, you will be driven out of all the exercise
of faith by an unfavorable providence.

I will give you two instances of this in Hebrews 11.
The first is that of father Abraham in verses 8–9: "By
faith Abraham, when he was called to go out into a
place which he should after receive for an inheritance,
obeyed; and he went out, not knowing whither he went.
By faith he sojourned in the land of promise, as in a
strange country, dwelling in tabernacles with Isaac and
Jacob, the heirs with him of the same promise." Here
Abraham was called to leave the possessions of his natural place, the possessions that he was born to, and to
follow Christ wherever He would lead him, to accept
that condition which Christ would place him in, and to
accept the allowance of God, let it be more or less. Now,
it is said, Abraham by faith obeyed this command and
call of God, and went out. Why, how did faith help him
here? Doubtless, by showing him Christ Jesus; for faith
in every exercise has to do with Christ. And, therefore,
his faith carried him up to Christ. Then, behold, how
low were these things to him! "Lord, my country?" he
said. "What is my country to Thee? I will leave my country to follow Thee. My friends are nothing to me, and
my possessions are nothing to me. I will leave all to follow Thee." See what a low esteem he had of these
things.

The other instance is that of Moses, in verses 24–26.
"By faith Moses, when he was come to years, refused to
be called the son of Pharaoh's daughter, choosing
rather to suffer affliction with the people of God than
to enjoy the pleasures of sin for a season, esteeming the
reproach of Christ greater riches than the treasures in
Egypt; for he had respect unto the recompense of the

reward." Here are great things that Moses left for the sake of Christ: he left the court, yea, he probably left the crown of Egypt and all the glories thereof. Now, he did this by faith; material things were of a low esteem with him. "Alas, what is it to be called the son of Pharaoh's daughter, and what is it to be the heir of an earthly crown, and to be king of Egypt? I would rather be afflicted, spoiled, and destitute in my outward condition with Christ than to enjoy all these things without Him."

Christians, you must mortify your affections for all enjoyments on this side of Christ, if you would come to live upon and glory in Christ alone.

DIRECTION 2. Acquaint yourselves more with the royalties of Christ, and the greatness of His gospel glory, as He is proposed as the object of your faith, if you would come to glory in Him alone and live upon Him in an empty condition.

One great reason why we can take no more comfort in Christ in an empty condition is that we are such strangers to the fullness of Christ Jesus. We do not know what is in Christ; we do not know what He can do, what is in His heart and hand to give forth to us. Christians, if you would live more by faith in Christ, then view Him in His royalties of grace; look into the length and the breadth of Christ, and see what He is the owner and possessor of, what the Father has entrusted Him with. View the extent of His offices; consider the largeness of His power and what He is able to do for you. Study and acquaint yourselves with the royalties of Christ, as He is proposed as the object for your faith to fix upon. There is no condition but He can comfort you in it, let the condition be ever so comfortless in itself. Study, then, the fullness of the Lord Jesus.

DIRECTION 3. By faith, get upon the all-sufficiency of Christ, and there take a view of your losses and of your troubles, and then you will see them to be but small.

You go, Christians, and stand below Christ, and there you look upon your troubles and afflictions; and then indeed they seem very great. Well, but get upon the all-sufficiency of Christ, and then view them; get upon the mount, and look down upon all your losses and crosses, and they will seem little things then. "What is this loss that I have sustained compared to what I have in the Lord Jesus Christ? What is my poor, empty vessel compared to the great fullness that is in the ocean of the Lord Jesus?" If you stood upon the all-sufficiency of Christ, and looked upon the disasters of your outward condition, they would seem to be like a little vessel brought to the great sea; the vessel is at once filled, and yet there is no lessening of the water in the ocean, but the sea is as full as ever.

DIRECTION 4. Always keep the invisible things of Christ's grace and of Christ's glory in your eye.

This is something strange, but it is the mystery of faith. I say, keep invisible things in your eye. Faith knows the meaning of it; faith will spy an invisible thing. That which sense can discern nothing of, faith will espy and keep sight of. Now, this was one way that Moses used in order to bring himself to live upon the Lord Jesus by faith: he kept invisible things in his eye; he saw Him who was invisible. Hebrews 11:27: "He endured, as seeing Him Who is invisible." And what is the description that the apostle gives of faith in a gospel exercise that we are speaking of but that which I have told you, the discerning of invisible things? "Now, faith is the substance of things hoped for, the evidence of things not seen" (Hebrews 11:1). Faith in its exercise will ransack among the promises, the promises of both grace and glory, and there will spy a great treasure, and show it to the soul as that which is his and belongs to him.

Now, Christian, view the promises of grace and of glory that are in the hands of Jesus Christ, and see the invisible graces, the invisible comforts, and the invisible blessings that are contained in them, and never lose the sight of these invisible things. Keep them always in your eye, and then you will see a glorious Jesus whom your souls will love to dwell upon, and you will not dwell away from Him.

DIRECTION 5. Never ground your faith and your hope upon your experience, but upon the promises, which are always attended with a wonderful working power.

If you ground your faith and your hope upon your experiences, then if your second trial is greater than your first, your faith will be perplexed, and you will sit down under discouragement. Indeed, there is a holy and Christian use that is to be made of your experiences, but you must never ground your faith and hope upon them; for God is always an outdoing God. He will outdo His own act. He will go further in one act than He will in another. If you ground your faith upon your experiences, when you come into a new strait that you never came into before, your faith will fail.

Consider the Israelites. If they had gone no further than their experiences, what a loss they would have been in! Nay, upon this account they were at a great loss; they only considered what God had done for them, and did not consider what He could do, and what a boundless power was working through the promise for them. Therefore, though they were delivered through the Red Sea, yet they said, "Can God spread a table in the wilderness? Moses, what, hast thou brought us into the wilderness to destroy us? There is no bread here, there is no water here, how can we subsist?" (see Psalm 78:19; Exodus 16:3). They never had experienced the wonders of God's power in those particular cases, and, therefore, their experiences could not carry them through. But they were to exercise faith upon the promise that had a boundless power working with it, and that would have told them that God can spread a table in the wilderness, and can command a rock to give out water for the Israelites' necessity. Let the history of the Lord's dealings with them tell you that there is no strait too great for Christ Jesus to deliver you out of. Faith in the promise will tell you that you have never experienced or seen the utmost end of Christ's power yet; you have never seen into the midst of His treasures of grace. You have seen but a little way. Faith in the promise will tell you this; therefore, never ground your faith and hope upon your experiences, though they have been large, but upon the promises, which have always a boundless power working with them.

DIRECTION 6. Consider that it is your duty to come and claim the grace of Christ, and plead with God for help on the ground of your interest in Christ Jesus according to your every need.

I say, if you would live by faith upon the Lord Jesus, then claim the grace of your interest according to the special need you feel at any time. Sirs, do you have an interest in Christ Jesus? Then Christ Jesus is yours; and all that He has is yours, and for you (1 Corinthians 3:21–23). Now, if you would live by faith upon Him, then come and put in your claim, and say, "The power of Jesus Christ is mine, and the grace of Jesus Christ is mine. He is for me. He is under special promise to me, and He is under peculiar engagement to me. He is mine to live upon. I will lean upon the arm of the Lord's strength, and I will glory in His fullness as a supply for my own emptiness."

There must be in the exercise of faith a peculiar claim that the soul must lay unto Christ, and a peculiar improving of the fullness of His interest, according to the emptiness of your state. And thus, Christians, you may be supported, whatever you meet with in this world. Suppose you sustain a loss. Why, in a fresh application to Christ you will have it made up in Him; and if a great failure and disappointment should come upon you, in a renewed act of faith upon the Lord Jesus Christ, applying something of His fullness and sweetness, you will have your condition filled. And so, as it is emptied in the creature, it will be filled with grace, and with Christ.

DIRECTION 7. If you would live by faith upon Christ, so as to receive joy and comfort from Him in every condition, then labor to bring your will to be content with your condition or lot in this world; keep your spirit within the confines of the will of God under all the various disposals of providence.

The recoiling and clashing of our will with our condition is a main hindrance unto our rejoicing in and acing faith upon the Lord Jesus under a sad providence. And the great reason why some persons are under such great dissatisfaction in their own spirits, and do not know how to bear the troubles of their state, is that their wills are not brought to their condition. Rather, they go about to bring their condition to their wills, and when anything considerable comes upon them that does not suit their wills, it causes disquiets, disturbances of spirit, and discomposure of heart—and such a soul will never rejoice in Christ in an evil day.

Now, Christians, if you would live the life of faith, you must bring your will to be content with your condition or lot in this world, be it what it may. Own the disposing hand of God that makes the change, whatever your change is; yield obedience to the Lord's will, that has the overruling power of your state, and keep your spirits within the confines of the will of God. Otherwise a cross or a trial in your outward condition will make a great alteration in the inward frame of your spirit.

I will give you a few instances in order to make this plain to you.

Paul was a man who rejoiced and gloried in Christ Jesus when he had hardly anything else left to him in this world. Many times his heart was made sad by the churches of Christ that he came to make glad (see 2 Corinthians 2:1–4). As to losses, who met with more? Said Paul, "I was in perils oft, and in hunger, and in distress, and in nakedness" (see 2 Corinthians 11:23–30). And yet this man gloried in tribulations; he counted it all joy when he fell into divers tribulations (James 1:2). How did it come about that this man was rejoicing in Christ Jesus (Philippians 2:16–18; 4:4) when the whole world frowned upon him? He tells us that his will was brought unto his condition. "I speak not in respect of want; for I have learned, in whatsoever state I am, therewith to be content. I know both how to be abased, and how to abound" (Philippians 4:11–12). He said, "If God empties me, my will is brought to my condition. I am willing to be emptied; if the Lord will make me poor, and take away what I have, I am willing to be made poor; my spirit is brought to my condition." He who can live in the confines of the will of God will live comfortably, and will rejoice in the Lord at all times.

Another instance of this is Job. Job, you know, was a man who was sorely tried, I suppose as much as ever a man was upon earth. Now, Job's will was brought to his condition; and hence he came to rejoice in the Lord (Job 1:21). But Job's wife's spirit was not brought to her condition; she could not tell how to be contented, for she said unto him, "Dost thou still retain thine integrity? Curse God and die." But he said unto her, "Thou speakest as one of the foolish women speaketh. What! shall we receive good at the hand of God, and shall we not receive evil?" (Job 2:9–10). It is as if he had said, "It was the Lord who filled me, and shall not the Lord empty me? We were satisfied when the Lord was filling us, and shall we not be satisfied now that the Lord is emptying us?"

Another instance is that of good old Eli. "Samuel told him every whit, and hid nothing from him. And he said, 'It is the Lord; let Him do what seemeth Him good' " (1 Samuel 3:18). "If the Lord will strip me," Eli thought, "I am willing to be stripped; if the Lord will take away my children, take away my comforts, and break up my house, it is the Lord. I am contented; if the Lord will do so, let Him; my will is brought to my condition. Let Him do what seemeth Him good."

So David (2 Samuel 15:26): "But if He thus say, 'I have no delight in thee,' behold, here am I, let Him do to me as seemeth good unto Him."

And thus it was with our Lord Jesus, the greatest instance of all: "Father, not My will, but Thine be done" (Luke 22:42). "Let My Father choose for Me. I will not bring My will into competition with His. If He will have Me drink of this cup, I will drink it; if He will have Me lay down My life, I will; if He will have all my glory obscured, it shall be so; if He will have Me be a man of sorrows, His will be done, and not My will."

You do not know, Christians, what an alteration of heart and life this living in subjection to the will of God will make.

DIRECTION 8. Take captive, and throw out all the suggestions of sense and reason upon the rising difficulties of your state.

If you allow reason to speak to your hearts when you are in some difficulty, or sense to rule your spirits, the result will be to cause you to repine and murmur, and to sin against God. Sense and reason are great enemies unto our peace and comfort. If sense and reason have liberty to speak, and to be heard in your hearts, they will certainly lay your spirits under a discouragement, and drive you off from the Lord.

Thus it was with Israel when they were in the wilderness: as soon as they had come out of Egypt, where they had their rivers and their pools and their ponds of water, and where they had their fleshpots and were fed to the full, they came into a howling wilderness, into a dry and barren place, where they had no wells of water, where there was no plowing or sowing. Then they fell into murmuring against and chiding of Moses, and said, "Why have you brought us into this place to slay us? For it is not supposed to be rational that we can live here in this wilderness. But if we abide here we will die." Numbers 11:4–5: "And the mixed multitude that was among them fell to lusting: and the children of Israel also wept again, and said, 'Who shall give us flesh to eat? We remember the fish which we did eat in Egypt freely, the cucumbers and the melons.' " "Yea, they spake against God; they said, 'Can God furnish a table in the wilderness?' " (Psalm 78:19). And "There was no water for the congregation; and they gathered themselves together against Moses and against Aaron. And the people chided Moses, and spake, saying, 'Would to God that we had died when our brethren died before the Lord! And why have ye brought up the congregation of the Lord unto this wilderness, that we and our cattle should die there? And wherefore have ye made us to come up out of Egypt, to bring us in unto this evil place? It is no place of seed, or of figs, or of vines, or of pomegranates' " (Numbers 20:2–5).

Here you see that sense and reason spoke over their condition, and you see how it laid their souls under discouragement. And if you do but review, at your leisure, the great murmurings of this people when they were in the wilderness, you will see that it was something or other that sense and reason suggested to them under some providence or other that disquieted their spirits.

It was through the suggestion of sense and reason that Zechariah questioned the truth of the word of God sent to him by the angel about having a son. "And Zechariah said unto the angel, 'Whereby shall I know this? For I am an old man, and my wife well stricken in years' " (Luke 1:18).

It was from the instigation of sense and reason that the unbelieving lord questioned that great plenty which the prophet told him would come the next day: 2 Kings 7:1–2: "Thus saith the Lord, 'Tomorrow about this time shall a measure of fine flour be sold for a shekel, and two measures of barley for a shekel, in the gate of Samaria.' Then a lord, on whose hand the king leaned, answered the man of God, and said, 'Behold, if the Lord would make windows in heaven, might this thing be?' " He only argued upon the prophecy in his own reason and in his own sense; and this made him so unbelieving as to reject the prophecy of the prophet.

This sense and reason made the disciples themselves question the intention of the Lord about feeding so great a multitude as there was with such small provision as they had. "In those days the multitude being very great, and having nothing to eat, Jesus called His disciples unto Him, and saith unto them, 'I have compassion on the multitude, because they have now been with Me three days, and have nothing to eat' " (Mark 8:1–2). His disciples said unto Him, "From whence can a man satisfy these men with bread here in the wilderness?" (verse 4).

So if you would get into this life of faith, keep down sense and reason, and cast out their suggestions, which will not bring you near to, but will set you further off from, the Lord. Do not say, upon a new difficulty, "There is no way to escape," or, upon a loss, "This or that is gone, and can never be made up to me again." But throw out the reasonings of sense; for if the discouraging suggestions of sense are resisted and set aside, faith will then get up and speak to the heart.

DIRECTION 9. Look through and beyond the discouragements of second causes unto the encouragements of the First Cause, who is always absolute and independent, and there fix your eye in every difficulty.

Second causes are fallible, but the First Cause is not, who is the efficient cause of all. And the Lord, who is the First Cause and the efficient cause of all, oftentimes dries up all creature streams, and causes visible human help to fail, so that we may see how great He is. Though the Lord ordinarily makes use of second causes, yet the Lord will so walk towards us, to reveal to us that He is not tied to means, that He is not tied to second causes. He oftentimes causes visible helps to fail so that our eyes may be upon Him as the first, absolute, independent Cause of all.

I will give you an instance of this, and it is that of Israel. Israel was in the way of the Lord, marching towards the land of promise; and the Lord took them into the wilderness brought them to the mouth of the Red Sea. Now, all second causes failed for help; there was not a ship nor a boat to carry the hosts of Israel over the water. But the First Cause was in no difficulty; and, therefore, said Moses, from the Lord, "Stand still, and see the salvation of the Lord" (Exodus 14:13). Now, do not let your eyes be upon the second cause, but upon the First Cause, and you shall see what a deliverance God can make for you. He carried all the hosts of Israel, men, women, and children, through the drowning sea, and not a man, woman, or child was lost in the passage, and yet there was neither ship nor boat to aid them over. And afterwards, when they came to the Jordan, the waters were before them and there was no boat to bear them over the waters, but the Lord commanded Israel to go on, and the waters made way for them. The waters rose up ins a heap, and Israel had a path made in the great deep (see Joshua 3:9–17).

I will now give you an instance of a good man, a man of great faith, and that was Moses. Moses, in a considerable difficulty, fixed his eye upon the second cause and pored over the discouragements it presented and was tossed in his spirit by not looking beyond it unto the First Cause, and the encouragements that the First Cause administered. The story is found in Numbers 11:19–21. The people, in the preceding verses, murmured against Moses because they had no flesh to eat. They had come from their full tables in Egypt, and they did not now have their dainties to live upon, and they did not know now how to be content. "Why," said God, "you shall not eat one day, nor two, but even a whole month." Now, read what Moses said in verses 21–22: "The people among whom I am are six hundred thousand footmen; and Thou hast said, 'I will give them flesh, that they may eat a whole month.' Shall the flocks and the herds be slain for them, to suffice them? Or shall all the fish of the sea be gathered together for them to suffice them?" Here is the history. God told this whole congregation that they would have flesh to eat for a month; they would eat and be satisfied; they would eat till they could eat no more. But Moses had his eye fixed upon second causes, and not upon the First Cause, and so he questioned this. "Lord," said he, "how can this be? So many hundred thousands of us; and what! shall we all have flesh to eat?"

Now, on the other hand, we read of Asa, when a mighty host of one million came out against him; he looked beyond the discouragements of second causes unto the encouragements of the First Cause, who is absolute and independent. And mark how this spirit held up: "And Asa cried unto the Lord his God, and said, 'Lord, it is nothing with Thee to help, whether with many, or with them that have no power; help us, O Lord our God; for we rest on Thee, and in Thy name we go against this multitude' " (2 Chronicles 14:11). He looked unto God, the First Cause of all, and he saw that the power of God was enough to charge this whole army, and to engage against this great multitude that came out against him.

And this was the prophet's spirit, and the course that he took here in the hour. All second causes failed, frowned, and administered only discouragement; the fig tree did not blossom, there was no fruit in the vines, the labor of the olive failed, the fields yielded no meat. The flocks were cut off from the fold, and there was no herd in the stall. Here was a failure of all second causes; now, he said, "I will look unto the First Cause, I will rejoice in the Lord, I will joy in the God of my salvation (Habakkuk 3:17–18).

Christians, let me tell you that if you lay the weight of your case upon second causes you will never come to rejoice in Christ Jesus in a difficulty. Remember, therefore, that when such a stream is dried up the Fountain is still full, and the Fountain can send out more ways than one. The Fountain that issued out a stream in such a place can issue out a stream in another place. As long as the Fountain is full, there is no fear of want; and if you would come to live upon the Lord Jesus Christ in a difficulty, you must keep your eye upon the Fountain that is ever full and that overflows.

DIRECTION 10. If you would live by faith upon Jesus Christ so as to fetch joy and comfort from Him under

the saddest providences of your state, then consider the
unchangeable love of Jesus Christ that metes out and
manages unto blessed ends all the losses, crosses, trials,
and tribulations of your state.

The hard thoughts that we have of our troubles, and
the hard thoughts that we have of the Lord when we are
troubled, drive us off from Him and lay our spirits under great discouragements. "What!" says the soul, "live
upon Jesus Christ and rejoice in Him? How can I do
that when He comes out against me as my enemy? He
writes bitter things against me. He is undoing me. He
is breaking and spoiling me; and can I rejoice in Him?"
The hard thoughts that the Church had of the Lord
was that which so overwhelmed her spirit when she
came into a low condition. Psalm 77:8–9: "His mercy is
clean gone, and He hath forgotten to be gracious. He
will be merciful to me no more. His mercies are shut
up, and fail for evermore. And how can we now rejoice
in this Lord?"

Now, all this while you do not understand the Lord
nor the design of the Lord; and by your ignorance you
come to wrong your own spirits in your present condition by giving way to a feeling of discouragement,
which, if you rightly understood the dealings of the
Lord, you would know was not the purpose of His providence in this matter. For do but consider that there is
unchangeable love engaged in and mixed with every
adverse providence. The Lord both strikes and wounds
in a way of love. He breaks in upon this or that comfort
and makes breaches in your condition, in a way of love
and grace. The Lord takes away a creature comfort from
a Christian to make more room in his heart for Christ.
The Lord puts him into the furnace so that He may pu-

rify him from his dross. The Lord purges him to make him a partaker of His holiness (Hebrews 12:10). The Lord shakes him from every feeling of confidence and comfort in the things of this life so that he might take faster hold upon Christ Jesus.

The Lord sends out every tribulation upon you with a charge to do you good and to use you kindly. When David sent out his army he gave them a charge: "Deal gently for my sake with the young man Absalom" (2 Samuel 18:5). So says Jesus Christ unto every cross that befalls you, "Use My servant kindly for My sake; treat him well." The Lord says unto any loss, "Work for the gain of such a servant of Mine." The Lord says unto such a cross, "You try, you refine, you purge, and you improve My servant." Unto such a tribulation He says, "Go and do such servants of Mine good."

There is unchangeable love and grace that metes out and manages unto blessed ends all the crosses of your condition. "Behold, happy is the man whom God correcteth; therefore, despise not thou the chastening of the Almighty" (Job 5:17). We say, "Crossed is the man, broken is the man, and undone is the man, who is thus dealt with." But God says, "Happy is the man." There is a blessing under the cross; there are love and grace in the trial which you do not consider, Christian. And this will be more advantageous to you than all the disadvantages that the cross can bring in upon you, in itself considered. "For whom the Lord loveth, He correcteth, even as a father the son in whom he delighteth" (Proverbs 3:12).

So then there is love in all the Lord's corrections. And so Isaiah 48:10: "Behold, I have refined thee, but not with silver. I have chosen thee in the furnace of affliction." The Lord says, "I have put you into the furnace; there is My love working towards you; there is my love speaking to you, refining, purging, and purifying you to make you more excellent gold for My use." This is the design of the Lord. "And ye have forgotten the exhortation which speaketh unto you as unto children, 'My son, despise not thou the chastening of the Lord, nor faint when thou art rebuked of Him; for whom the Lord loveth He chasteneth, and scourgeth every son whom He receiveth' " (Hebrews 12:5–6). "As many as I love, I rebuke and chasten" (Revelation 3:19). "Who shall separate us from the love of Christ? Shall tribulation, or distress, or persecution, or famine, or nakedness, or peril, or sword?" (Romans 8:35). None of these things shall do it, He says. So if you would come to rejoice in the Lord in a trying hour, consider the unchangeable love of Jesus Christ, who metes out and manages the crosses which you are called to bear. "It was good for me," said the Psalmist, "that I was afflicted" (Psalm 119:71). And again, "I believed, therefore have I spoken; I was greatly afflicted. I said in my haste, 'All men are liars.' What shall I render unto the Lord for all His benefits?" (Psalm 116:10–12).

Surely the prophet did not have only removing the affliction in mind, but also the design of God in the affliction, when he said, "What shall I render unto the Lord for all His benefits? I will take the cup of salvation" (see Psalm 116:13), "and bless His name. though He has greatly afflicted me and sorely distressed me." Doubtless, he had respect unto the design. Well, if you would come to live rejoicingly in the Lord in all conditions, consider His unchangeable love that both orders and disposes the trials that exercise you.

DIRECTION 11. Consider the relationship that Christ stands in to your souls, and the grace that is dispensed to you as a result of this relationship.

You look, Christians, in an evil day, below the comforts of your state; and that is the reason why you are so hurried in your own spirits. You pore over an emptying providence, and do not consider the satisfying relationship that Christ has unchangeably entered into with your souls. This is a relationship of grace that is always comforting and always relieving, and that has new supplies of grace always springing up in it for your assistance.

I will say a little regarding some aspects of this relationship.

• He is the Father of believers. The Lord Jesus Christ is called by that name in Isaiah 9:6: "Unto us a child is born, unto us a Son is given . . . and His name shall be called Wonderful, Counselor, the mighty God, the everlasting Father." So Isaiah 8:18: "Behold, I and the children whom the Lord hath given Me are for signs and for wonders in Israel." "Behold, I and the children"— we are the Lord's children. And Isaiah 63:16: "Doubtless Thou art our Father, though Abraham be ignorant of us, and Israel acknowledge us not. Thou, O Lord, art our Father, our Redeemer; Thy name is from everlasting." This is spoken of Christ Jesus. Now, the relationship of a father is a relationship of pity; it is a relationship of love; it is a relationship of tenderness. When the Lord tells us that He stands in this relationship to us, He tells us that He will exercise the tenderness, the pity, and the kindness of a father unto this child. Now a tender-hearted father, will consider his child in all conditions and in all his straits; and though it is a rebellious child, yet still he will consider it, and he will exercise the pity and the tenderness of a father toward it.

This you may see in the conduct of David toward Absalom. Absalom was a rebellious son who proclaimed war against his father and would have cut him off. Yet see how David's heart yearned for his rebellious son when he heard that he was dead: "O Absalom, my son, my son, would to God I had died for thee! O Absalom, my son, my son!" (2 Samuel 18:33). Now, if there is so much tenderness in a human father towards his children, much more in Christ towards His children. Christ says, "If ye, being evil, know how to give good gifts unto your children, how much more shall your heavenly Father give the Holy Spirit to them that ask Him?" (Luke 11:13). Why, fathers in the flesh cannot outlove Jesus Christ. They do not have a larger heart for their children than Christ has for His.

• He is the Husband of believers. Now, that is a relationship of great care and tenderness. Oh, the faithful, wise, able, loving husband will defend his wife, provide for his wife, safeguard his wife, and pity his wife! In all her exigencies she will be as his own soul. "So ought men to love their wives as their own bodies. He that loveth his wife loveth himself. For no man ever yet hated his own flesh . . . this is a great mystery, but I speak concerning Christ and the Church" (Ephesians 5:28–29, 32). So all believers are betrothed and married unto Jesus Christ; and Jesus Christ, as a loving, able, wise, tender-hearted Husband, will secure, defend, and provide for those who are married to Him much more than the earthly husband can do for their wives.

• He is the Brother of believers. Jesus Christ is our

elder Brother. Now, a brother under the law was not to see any of his younger brethren in a decayed and low condition without relieving them. "If thy brother be waxen poor, and fall into decay, then thou shalt relieve him," was a Scripture law (Leviticus 25:35). Now, Christ says, "I am not ashamed to call them brethren" (Hebrews 2:11). And He will be a most loving, tender-hearted, faithful Brother unto all His brethren, whatever their straits and their trials are.

Oh, Christians, I pray you, weigh well and receive by faith what God reveals to you of the aiding, relieving, helpful relationships of grace that Christ stands in to your souls. Receive them, I say, by faith, and exercise your faith upon them. Do you sometimes think, "What if I had such a father, so wise, so able, so loving, so tender-hearted? How would my heart rejoice in him!" Why, Christians, you have all that you can imagine in Christ as a Father to you! But you say, "If I had such a tender husband, such a kind-hearted husband, how would I take comfort in him." Christian, you have all in Christ Jesus that you can imagine, and much more abundantly. Imagine the most loving, faithful brother there ever was on the earth; you have more in Christ Jesus than can be imagined. Christ stands in all these relationships to you, and these relationships are obligations for Him. According to these relationshipships will He act and dispense, and according to the obligation of every relationship shall the dispensation be. So He is not only a Husband, but you may believe that He will do all for you (since you are betrothed to Him) that the relationship of a Husband obliges Him to. He will do all as a Father for you that the relationship obliges Him to, and He will do all as a Brother that the relationship binds Him to.

Know further, Christians, that you can never outlive the love and the grace of the relationships of Christ, neither can you overburden the love of any of His relationships; you can never overcharge His love. There is a natural love arising in the heart of a father towards his children, a growing, springing love every day, so that, notwithstanding many provocations, still the father keeps his heart upon his child. Thus, though there are provocations between you and your heavenly Father, yet His heart is kept towards you. His heart is the heart of a Father. His heart is the heart of a Husband, and His heart is the heart of a Brother—and you can never overburden His love, nor outlive His grace, nor over-believe the fullness of these relationships of grace that He stands in to your souls. Now, then, if you would come to an exercise of faith upon the Lord Jesus Christ, then consider the auxiliary relationships of grace that He stands in to your souls, and what is dispensable upon those relationships, and wait upon Him for the fulfillment of all.

DIRECTION 12. If you would come to live a life of faith upon Christ Jesus, rejoicing in Him under any strait and trial of providence, then take up a promise, and believe it upon the bare faithfulness of God, and never dispute with the difficulty or apprehended impossibility of it.

There are sometimes great mountains of difficulty that lie before the promise; you must not consult with these, Christians, but consult with the promises as they are in the hands of the faithfulness of God, and believe the truth of every promise because God has spoken it, however unlikely and improbable unto sense and reason the accomplishment of it is. Do not say, "How can this be? How can such a promise be fulfilled? It is not likely that it should be fulfilled to me, since it is so unsuitable and so unanswerable." But look to the faithfulness of God who made the promise, and believe it upon God's bare truth, because He hath spoken it, when you have nothing else to encourage you to take it up.

Thus it was with Abraham, the father of believers, "who against hope believed in hope . . . and being not weak in faith, he considered not his own body now dead, when he was about a hundred years old, neither yet the deadness of Sarah's womb" (Romans 4:18–19). There was an unlikelihood of this promise ever being fulfilled; and if Abraham had reasoned according to sense, it would have suggested to him that this promise was a mere fallacy, a mere romance, that there was no truth or certainty in it. What! he a hundred years old, a dead man almost, his nature quite decayed, and Sarah even going into the grave, almost a dead woman, nature quite decayed in her; and what! shall Sarah conceive and have a son? It is not likely or probable. "Nay," says reason, "it is an impossible thing." Now, there would have been a discouragement to his spirit if he had called in sense and reason, and considered and debated the matter therewith; but he took up the promise, and believed it upon the bare word of God, upon His bare faithfulness. "Well," said Abraham, "I am, indeed, an old man, and Sarah, my wife, is an old woman. But God has said I shall have a child, and I believe it. There is no hope in nature, but I will believe it against hope, against all discouragement of my hope. I will believe that God, who has spoken it, is able to perform it. Surely, then, it shall be so."

Thus, Christians, when difficulties and discouragements encompass the promise, do not dispute with the difficulties that lie in the way. But keep your eye upon the faithfulness of God, and believe the promise upon God's bare word alone.

DIRECTION 13. Take the promise that is suitable to your present state, whatever it may be, and place it alongside your trial or your temptation, and then wait upon the Lord for the accomplishment of the promise.

I say, single out a promise suitable to your state and set it at the head of your trial, at the mouth of your trouble or temptation, and then wait upon the Lord for the accomplishment of the promise. You can be brought into no condition but there is some promise in the New Testament that suits your trial, whatever it is; there is no burden laid upon your back but some promise suits the burden. Now, you must select a promise suitable to your present state and set it at the head of your trial; keep your eye there, waiting for the accomplishment of the promise, and hereby your hearts will be raised up to glory and will rejoice in the Lord alone.

Suppose that you are in some considerable danger; select some gospel delivering promise, and set it at the head of your danger. Suppose, Christian, that you have some great burden upon your spirit; choose some soul-reviving promise and set it at the head of your burden. Suppose that you have met with some extraordinary loss; select some comforting, reviving promise, some promise of supplies that Jesus Christ has made, and set that at the door where your comfort went out; keep your eye upon the promise of your state and the promise of your present condition, and wait upon the Lord for its accomplishment. By this means your heart will, in a little time, come to be raised, and you will see a new supply ready to come in upon your empty condition.

DIRECTION 14. Keep the communicable attributes of Christ before your view as under an unchangeable reconciliation and obligation unto you.

My friends, if Christ is yours, then all of Christ is yours. When Christ gave you an interest in Himself, He gave all of Himself to you. All the attributes of His eternal, glorious nature are engaged to you; they are reconciled to you, and they are under an express gospel covenant obligation to you. Now, consider these and keep them in your view. Consider that the power of Jesus Christ is under engagement for you. Consider that the wisdom of Christ Jesus is engaged to you. I speak to every believer in particular, for Christ gives Himself over as fully to one believer as if He had but one believer to give Himself to. The faithfulness of Christ Jesus is engaged to you; the love and the grace of Christ Jesus are engaged to you.

Now, Christians, if you would come to rejoice in Christ, then often consider these things; propose these attributes as under a special, unchangeable covenant of reconciliation and obligation to you. Consider also how much there is in every property of His nature. Do but consider how much there is in the power of Christ; how much there is in the love of Christ; how much there is in the grace of Christ; how much there is in the wisdom of Christ.

Christians, there is a fountain in every attribute of Christ. There is a fountain of power in Christ's attribute of power; there is a fountain of love in Christ's attribute of love; there is a fountain of grace in Christ's attribute of grace; and these fountains are set open for every Christian. Do but see, then, how many fountains you have to go to. You complain of want and emptiness, that you have nothing; why, here are full fountains to go unto, all of which are set open at all times for your relief.

O Christian, do but propose these to your consideration, and your heart will soon leap out to rejoice in the Lord.

DIRECTION 15. If you would come to live by faith upon the Lord Jesus in all conditions, then reckon that your all is in Christ, and is always sure in Christ, though some outward comforts of your condition are coming and going.

Jesus Christ is the possessor of your blessedness; your blessedness is not in your own hand, nor in the hands of a stranger, but in the hands of Christ. And the outward comforts of your condition are not your portion, Christians; they are not your all, but your all lies in Christ. When you have lost an estate, your all is still sure in the hands of Christ. When you have lost a friend or a relative, your all is still in the hands of Christ, untouched. There it is, and it is always sure in the hand where it is lodged. Now, do but reckon that your comforts lie here, and that the Lord is the keeper and possessor of all your hopes, of all your blessings and blessedness, of all your comforts and consolations, of your whole treasure, and your souls will come to be drawn out after Christ to rejoice in Him.

The apostle says in Colossians 3:11, "But Christ is all and in all." He sums up all in a few words: all is in Christ. Why, then, you who have an interest in Christ, reckon that your all lies there, and then will your souls be enlarged to look towards Him.

In closing, I might add that you should look up unto God the Father, in the sense of your weakness in faith or lack of it, to increase your faith or to give you faith. The disciples went to Christ and said, "Lord, increase our faith" (Luke 17:5). So, Christians, should you do. It is an evil day, a trying day; it is by faith only that you will stand, and it is faith that will keep up your spirits. Oh, pray unto the Lord that He would increase your faith! Pray for the increase of this grace above all, and be earnest with Him, that He who has been the author would be the promoter of your faith.

And for your encouragement, Christians, let me tell you that:

1. The more you believe in Christ Jesus, the more you will glorify Christ.

Every act of faith glorifies Christ Jesus; it glorifies His fullness; it glorifies His all-sufficiency; it glorifies His advancement and enthronement at the right hand of the Father; it glorifies Him in His gospel offices, as He is entrusted with the fullness of all grace for you.

2. Believing in the Lord Jesus Christ engages Jesus Christ to come in for your help.

Every act of faith not only glorifies Him, but engages Him. It will awaken His power and cause Him to arise, open His hand, and give out more liberally and freely. He says, therefore, unto His servants, "According to your faith, be it unto you."

3. This living upon Jesus Christ is the only way to make your lives comfortable in this world.

What had the prophet Habakkuk to comfort his heart with except to rest upon the Lord Jesus Christ

alone? The fig tree was withered and his creature comforts were gone; emptiness and nothingness were before him. "Well," said he, "I will rejoice in the Lord. I
will joy in the God of my salvation." Behold, this is what
made his condition comfortable. Why, Christians, you
will never have comfort in your own spirits under a loss,
under a cross, or in a time of temptation, if you do not
exercise faith upon Christ Jesus and there fix your
souls.

4. Hereby you shall have confirmation, establish-
ment, and settlement in the greatest shakings of providence that may be brought upon your condition.

O Christian! Let me, in winding up all, once more
call upon you to live upon and glory in Christ Jesus
alone. As for all your comforts in this world, you cannot
promise yourself that they shall abide with you. God
may empty you from vessel to vessel till He has taken all
these away. But now there is enough in the Lord Jesus
alone to take comfort in; there is enough in Jesus
Christ alone for you to glory in.

Oh, come and draw your comforts from Christ, and
do not draw them from the creature. Do not draw them
from secondary helps, but draw them from the
Fountain; do not sit down at the streams, but get away
to the Fountain, to the Ocean that is always full! In every strait have your eye upon Jesus; in every cross keep
your eye upon Jesus; in every loss keep your eye upon
Jesus; under every strait and trial have recourse to Jesus,
and acquaint yourself more with Him, so that you may
be in the prophet's frame, rejoicing in the Lord and
joying in the God of your salvation.

Appendix 1

The Hope of the Saints in Heaven

"For the hope which is laid up for you in heaven,
whereof ye heard before in the word of the
truth of the gospel." Colossians 1:5

This holy apostle, being in bonds for the sake of Christ, understanding from Epaphras that this church with which he had taken great pains in the Lord was in danger of being carried off from the purity and simplicity of the gospel by some seducers and false teachers—who would set up the abrogated institutions of Moses alongside the institutions of Christ—makes it his business to confirm them in the faith that they had received.

After the inscription and salutation, the apostle gives thanks to the God and Father of our Lord Jesus Christ for what He had done for these people, and then declares how much they were upon his heart. He could not cease praying for them, and he rejoiced in their faith and love, as you may see in verses 3–4: "We give thanks to God and the Father of our Lord Jesus Christ, praying always for you, since we heard of your faith in Christ Jesus, and of the love which you have to all the saints." He then speaks of their hope in verse 5, saying that it is "laid up for you in heaven." By hope he does not mean the grace of hope, as it is sometimes to be taken in the Scriptures, but he means the object of hope, or the thing hoped for, as sometimes hope is to be understood, such as in Galatians 5:5: "For we through the Spirit wait for the hope of righteousness by faith." And Titus 2:13: "Looking for the blessed hope."

So the hope he speaks as laid up in heaven is heaven itself, and the glory and blessedness of it that belonged to those who had laid hold of Jesus, and upon eternal life in laying hold of Jesus. There are some who make these words dependent upon the preceding ones, and understand them to say, "We give thanks unto God for your faith and for your love, which are evidence that you have a hope that is laid up in heaven for you." Some others read these words, "We are rejoicing in your faith and in your love, which you have received, and wherein you stand fast, for the hope which is laid up for you in heaven." Some others understand the apostle to be expressing in verse 4 the causes and grounds of his giving thanks to God for them, and rejoicing on their account, and that is their faith and their love, which are illustrated in verse 5 in both their final and instrumental causes. The final cause is heaven and the blessedness thereof, which their faith and their love will issue in; the instrumental cause is the word of the truth of the gospel by which faith and love have been wrought in them, and by which they were made fit for the heavenly inheritance.

I intend to make only a short discourse upon the words. The proposition is this:

DOCTRINE: The saints have a hope which is laid up in heaven for them. They have the glory and the blessedness of heaven to feed and feast their expectations on while they are here. There is a world beyond this world where the saints have their treasure, where their great estate and their inheritance lie. They have some things here, but truly, as the apostle said in 1 Corinthians 15:19, "If in this life only we have hope in Christ, we are of all men most miserable." If there were nothing more than is to be enjoyed here, if they had nothing in reserve to mend their condition, they would have been poor indeed.

In John 16:33 Christ says, "In the world ye shall have tribulation." The saints have nothing but sorrows, trials, temptations, troubles, and afflictions here, but there is a glory that remains, a glory that is in reserve, that is to be revealed, that is another manner of inheritance than what is possessed and enjoyed by them here.

Colossians 3:3: "For ye are dead, and your life is hid with Christ in God." The life of the saints is a hidden life. God has hidden it from the world. He has hidden their estate. He has hidden their riches. He has hidden their glory from the world. They do not know what they are born and entitled to, but when Christ, who is our life, shall appear, then we shall also appear with Him in glory. As for the men of this world, you may see all that they have, for they have their all here. All that God intends to give them they possess here, and therefore they are called "men which have their portion in this life" (Psalm 17:14). And thus it is said of the rich man in Luke 16:25 that "he received his good things in this life." Abraham said, "Son, remember that you, in your lifetime, received your good things. You had your portion and your all here."

All the comfort, all the peace, all the honor, all the riches, and all the plenty that God ever intends to bestow upon wicked men, they have it here. But now, besides all that the saints have here, they have a hope which is laid up for them in heaven. They can look beyond and over things that are seen unto those things that are not seen, that is, by a carnal eye. They can look from present things that are perishing unto spiritual things that are eternal. 2 Corinthians 4:18: "While we look not at the things which are seen, but at the things which are not seen; for the things which are seen are temporal, but the things which are not seen are eternal."

We look at those things that are not seen, at the unseen things of another world. Romans 5:2: "We have access by faith into this grace wherein ye stand, and rejoice in hope of the glory of God." We have peace with God now, which is a foretaste of heaven let down into our hearts. But this is not all, we also rejoice in hope of the glory of God. Romans 8:17: "Being children we are heirs, heirs of God, and joint-heirs with Christ." Then Paul says that there is a glory to be revealed, one that all the sufferings of this life are not worthy to be compared with. 2 Timothy 4:8: "There is laid up for me a crown of righteousness, which the Lord, the righteous Judge, shall give me at that day, and not to me only, but to all them also that love His appearing." It is as if Paul is saying, "Now that I have fought the good fight, now that I have finished my course, now that I have come to the end of my journey, now that I am going out of the world and leaving all that I have here, there is a crown of righteousness in reserve for me, that is just ready to be set upon my head."

1 Peter 1:3–4: "Blessed be the God and Father of our Lord Jesus Christ, which according to His abundant mercy hath begotten us again unto a lively hope by the

resurrection of Jesus Christ from the dead, to an inheritance incorruptible and undefiled, which fadeth not away, reserved in heaven for you." It is not known what a saint is while he is here in this world, nor yet what a saint has, what he has in reversion, what he is called to, and what he shall be put into the possession of. 1 John 3:2: "Beloved, now are we the sons of God, and it doth not yet appear what we shall be, but we know that, when He shall appear, we shall be like Him, for we shall see Him as He is."

In speaking to this proposition, I shall show you what hope the saints have laid up in heaven for them. We shall glance a little at a few particulars to help your faith. But what the hope of a saint is, which is laid up in heaven for him, no man on earth is able to tell you. The apostle tells us in 2 Corinthians 2:9: "Eye hath not seen, nor ear heard, neither hath it entered into the heart of man to conceive what God hath prepared for them that love Him." And the Apostle Paul was taken up into the third heaven, and when he had come down he told us that the glory that was there, and the high and blessed enjoyments that are there, were unspeakable; he was not able to utter them. 1 Corinthians 12:4: "I was caught up into paradise, and heard unspeakable words, which it is not lawful for a man to utter." These were unspeakable words, inutterable words; he was not able to utter them when he had come down again. In verse 3 he says that whether he was in the body or out of the body he could not tell, but when he had come down again he was not able to tell what he heard and what he saw when he was transported. Yet there is something that the word of truth has made known to us to revive our spirits and strengthen our hope while we are on our journey. And some of those things I shall lay briefly before you.

1. In heaven, the saints shall have the perfection of all grace. Here they have grace, but grace is underage; grace is in a great deal of weakness; grace is mixed with a great deal of corruption. That is, there is a great deal of sin in the heart with grace. Grace does not stand alone in its full strength; grace here is so low and so little, so borne down and so often overtopped with corruption that it can hardly be seen by another; it can hardly be discerned by the persons themselves. A child of God is oftentimes at a loss to know what to make of his condition; he does not know whether he has any grace or not. Christ says, "O ye of little faith! Wherefore didst thou doubt?" (Matthew 14:31). The same may be said to us all: "O ye of little faith! O ye of little love! O ye of little patience! O ye of little humility! O ye of little self-denial!"

Grace is in a great deal of weakness here; grace indeed lies under a growing promise, and they who have received but a little receive it as the earnest of a great deal—but they have only the earnest here. But when they come to heaven they find perfection; all their graces are put into perfect strength. There will be no weakness in their love for God; there will be no shortcomings in their submission to the will of God. In that heavenly state, the saints are all advanced to a heavenly stature, even unto the measure of the stature of the fullness of Christ. Ephesians 4:13: "Till we all come in the unity of the faith, and of the knowledge of the Son of God, unto a perfect man, unto the measure of the stature of the fullness of Christ." Ephesians 5:27: "That He might present it to Himself a glorious church, not having spot or wrinkle, or any such thing, but that it should be holy and without blemish." There will be no weakness, no imperfection in the new man, but you shall be in your full-grown state in heaven immediately upon your translation. Therefore the souls of just men entering into heaven are said to be in a perfect state. Hebrews 12:23: "To the general assembly and church of the firstborn, which are written in heaven, and to God the Judge of all, and to the spirits of just men made perfect." Here you are glad to receive a little now and a little then, and to be adding by degrees. But there, grace shall be so complete that there shall be no room for a further degree, nor for a higher improvement.

2. The saints have a hope laid up in heaven of the glorification of these vile bodies. Our bodies are now full of corruption; they are earthly bodies, and they are a great clog and hindrance to a spiritual soul. But there shall come a change upon them. 1 Corinthians 15:42–44: "So also is the resurrection of the dead. It is sown in corruption, it is raised in incorruption. It is sown in dishonor, it is raised in glory. It is sown a natural body, it is raised a spiritual body."

Many are the corrupting diseases that our flesh is exposed to while we live. And such infections sometimes seize upon the body as to separate lovers and acquaintances far from them. But, to be sure, at death corruption seizes the body and makes it so loathsome that near relations cannot bear one another. Abraham cried out, "Oh, bury my dead out of my sight" (Genesis 23:4), and yet she was the wife of his bosom, bone of his bone and flesh of his flesh, for whom he lacked no love. Yet he wanted her buried out of his sight. The body is sown in dishonor, and indeed it lives so; for much of the glory, beauty, and fairness of the body of man that were at first bestowed upon him are lost. But all the scars, all the blemishes, and all the disfigurements of our bodies, all the effects of sin, shall at once be taken away. That which is sown in dishonor shall be raised in glory, that which is sown in weakness shall be raised in power, and that which is sown a natural body shall be raised a spiritual body. It shall be spiritual in its temperature, constitution, and complexion; it shall be spiritual in all its operations. It shall be raised to glory, and all the robes of mortality and all the rags of its vileness shall be left behind.

When Lazarus rose out of the grave, he arose with all his grave-clothes around him. He came with them out of his grave because he was to return again. John 11:44: "And he that was dead came forth bound hand and foot with grave-clothes." Jesus said to them, "Loose him and let him go." The grave was not done with him. This was not the blessed resurrection that was promised, but he came out of the grave to return again.

But when Jesus Christ arose out of the grave, He arose to return no more, and He left all His grave-clothes behind Him. John 20:6–7: "Then cometh Simon Peter, and went into the sepulcher, and seeth the linen clothes, and the napkin that was about His head." The grave-clothes, the napkin, and all that He had around Him were all left behind because He was to return no more.

Now Jesus arose as the first-fruits of the saints. 1 Corinthians 15:20: "But now is Christ risen from the dead, and become the first-fruits of them that slept." So you may see in the resurrection of Christ what shall happen to the saints in their resurrection. They shall leave all the clothes of their dishonor, their corruption, and their mortality behind them. Philippians 3:21: "These vile bodies of ours shall be changed, and made like unto the glorious body of Christ." He shall change our vile bodies, bodies full of corruption, full of weakness, bodies in so much dishonor; they shall be changed, and shall be fashioned like the glorious body of Christ. Romans 8:23: "And not only they, but ourselves also who have the first-fruits of the Spirit, even we ourselves groan within ourselves, waiting for the adoption, to wit, the redemption of our bodies."

So this is another part of the hope that is laid up in heaven for the saints, the glorification of their vile bodies. We shall have part of that glory and honor upon our bodies that the Father bestowed upon the body which He prepared for His Son when He took our nature. And truly the body of Jesus Christ in heaven is the most glorious creature that is there. It is a glory the saints shall admire forever. They shall not only admire it in Christ, but admire it in themselves, since they also shall be made partakers of it.

3. The saints have a hope laid up for them of an everlasting rest. There is no rest in this world; it is full of troubles and tossings to and fro, like a ship that is at sea in a storm. But in heaven there is rest: rest from all the troubles of men, rest from all the troubles of Satan, rest from all the troubles of sin. Sorrow shall flee from them. "All tears shall be wiped from their eyes" (Revelation 21:4). I shall not tell you here how far the saints may be made partakers of this that are promised on this side of heaven, but, to be sure, it is true of heaven itself. A saint would be glad to get into a corner where he might sit down and be at rest; but if he goes

out into the world, he is presently disturbed. If he goes into another place, he finds that his troubles follow him. His quarters are continually broken up; he can never be at rest, but one disquieting thing follows another, and one trouble takes another by the heels.

But in heaven the saints shall be taken into an everlasting rest. 2 Thessalonians 1:7: "And to you who are troubled, rest with us." Paul cheers up these Thessalonians under all the troubles that they met with from men and devils, and all the enemies in their way who were continually disquieting their spirits. "Well," he says, "cheer up; to you who are troubled, rest with us." Paul was abundant in labors, and abundant in sorrows and sufferings, but he comforted himself with the fact that there was a rest that remained for him. "And not for me only," he says, "but for you also; rest with us. You shall come into the same rest with us."

Ministers and people who are faithful in Christ Jesus shall all come into the same rest, a rest that none of the troublers shall be able to disturb. Revelation 14:13: "Blessed are the dead that die in the Lord from henceforth, yea, saith the Spirit, that they may rest from their labors; and their works do follow them." The labors and the pains that you take here are many. We were driven by God into this condition, in the sweat of our faces to eat our bread; but this is just for this life. You have a hope that is laid up in heaven for you of a blessed and glorious rest, wherein you shall have freedom from all your labors; you shall have freedom from all the disturbances and pressures you face here.

4. There is a fullness of joy that is laid up in heaven for all believers. Isaiah 66:11: "That ye may suck and be satisfied with the breasts of her consolation; that ye

may milk out and be delighted with the abundance of her glory." If there is such a time coming wherein this may be true of the saints here on earth, it will be much more so in heaven, for heaven will heighten all. It will heighten all your joy and all your comfort, and not only heighten the joy and comfort that you have, but that succeeding saints shall have when the whole earth shall be filled with the knowledge of the Lord. And yet still there shall be a disproportion between earth and heaven.

When the voice says, "Come up here," that which follows is, "Enter into your Master's joy" (Matthew 25:21). Here the Lord, to bear up the hearts of His people, sends down a little joy into their spirits. He sends down the Comforter to them, and He comes, and now and then speaks a reviving word; now and then He gives a drop of consolation. Perhaps it is upon the end of the rod sometimes, and this is counted a great matter; and truly it should be so with us. But there is a hope of another manner of joy laid up in heaven for you. Joy shall be the air that the saints shall breathe in; it shall be the very orb that they shall move in, the very elements that they shall dwell in. Their hearts cannot hold all; it shall be overflowing and it shall be round about them.

(1) The joy that is laid up in heaven for the saints will be fully satisfying. They shall have enough of it; they shall be filled with it to the full, so that there shall be no room for more. Psalm 16:11: "Thou wilt show me the path of life; in Thy presence is fullness of joy, and at Thy right hand are pleasures forevermore." But shall the saints have enough of this? Yes! Psalm 17:15: "As for me, I will behold Thy face in righteousness. I shall be

satisfied, when I awake, with Thy likeness." The soul
does not have its satisfaction here. When it has a little,
it is enlarged to bless God, but it does not have enough;
it would have more still, a little more communion with
God. But in heaven there is satisfaction to the full.
"When I awake"—that is, on the morning of the resurrection, when this mortality is blown out of his eyes—
when he comes to open his eyes in another world, then
shall he be "satisfied with Thy likeness."

(2) The joy that is laid up in heaven is unmixed.
Here there is a mixture with your joy. You have a little
joy and a great deal of sorrow; you have a little peace
and a great deal of trouble; you have darkness with your
light, and you have vexation and crosses with your comforts. But in heaven there is nothing to cross you; there
is nothing to grieve you; there is only joy, unmixed joy.
It will be pure joy.

(3) The joy that is laid up in heaven will be per-
manent. It is such as you shall sit down in, and that
which you shall partake of to all eternity. Here your joy
is not only mixed with sorrows, but it is sometimes
overwhelmed; it is coming and going; it is partaken of
here only with great uncertainties. But in heaven it will
always be the same.

5. There is in heaven laid up for you absolute freedom, and full liberty of soul in the service of God. Here
it is not so; when the spirit is willing, the flesh is
weak—and how often our hearts are ready to die within
us! The spirit will not hold out; we can hardly watch
with Christ one hour. Bodies tire as well as spirits. But
there will be a fullness of strength in heaven, and there
will be liberty of spirit proportionate to all strength and
to all grace. The soul will be in absolute freedom for

God, and the body will be under an absolute freedom too, answerable unto all the freedom of the soul. Now the body is a great clog to the soul; it is a great hindrance that you cannot do for God what you would and cannot lay yourselves out for God as you would; but there will be no weariness in heaven in your spirits, though you serve night and day, world without end. The promise is found in Isaiah 40:31: "They that wait upon the Lord shall renew their strength; they shall mount up with wings as eagles. They shall run and not be weary; they shall walk and not be faint."

The saints rejoice since they can experience something of this here, but the fullness of this promise will be in heaven. There you shall mount up indeed as with wings; there soul and body shall have all liberty in the service of God. What would saints give while on earth to have their spirits in full freedom and liberty for God for but one day! Oh, they would count it a corner of heaven if they could have their spirits at full liberty for God but for one day, that they may serve God and delight themselves fully in the service of God for a whole day. But, sirs, in heaven you shall be fully delighted in the service of God to all eternity; all clogs shall be taken off from your spirits.

6. The saints have a hope laid up in heaven for them of an eternal abode in the glorious palace of their Father. Here their dwelling is uncertain; they have no sure dwelling place on earth; their landlords sometimes put them out of their houses and command them to seek a new dwelling. Sometimes God turns them out of their houses here by the sword, or they may be driven out by fire, but the Lord has chosen heaven as the place of their perpetual residence. Deuteronomy 1:33: "Who

went in the way before you to search out a place." The
Lord went before Israel in the wilderness by fire and by
cloud to search out a place where His people should
dwell. Jesus, the Forerunner who has entered into
heaven, has gone before to search out a place, to
choose a place, and to prepare a place for you. John
14:2: "I go to prepare a place for you." And this place
that Christ has gone to prepare is in the Father's
house; there shall the saints' abode and dwelling be
forever. And there is no one who shall ever turn them
out of that house; but to all eternity they shall peaceably
possess it.

7. In heaven shall be the consummation of the marriage between Christ and believers. Here the marriage
is entered into. Christ and the believing soul are betrothed together. Hosea 2:19: "And I will betroth thee
unto Me forever." But the betrothal here is like when a
young man betroths a virgin: they live asunder after
they are betrothed. So Christ and your souls live asunder. You are betrothed here by grace, and you come together now and then in an ordinance; now and then
Christ lets out His heart unto you, and now and then
you let your hearts out to Christ; now and then Christ
sends you a token of His love, a letter of His love,
wherein He gives a manifestation of His love—but still
you are asunder. But in heaven the marriage shall be
consummated. 2 Corinthians 5:6: "While we are at
home in the body, we are absent from the Lord." We
live asunder, but when we come to depart, "we shall ever
be with the Lord" (1 Thessalonians 4:17). This is a
blessed day indeed, that will bring Jesus Christ and your
souls together, nevermore to be separated, nevermore
to be at a distance, never to be out of the presence of

one another again. Communion with God is sweet now, and when Jesus Christ lets out a little of Himself, the soul cries out, "Evermore give me of this Bread!" Here this communion is clouded and the sense of it can be lost; but when we come to be dissolved and to enter into heaven, then we shall be with the Lord.

8. The saints have a hope laid up for them in heaven of enjoying fellowship and society with all the sanctified ones in Christ Jesus. Heaven will bring all the saints together and keep them in an eternal communion. There are two things that the saints in heaven shall have: a full knowledge of one another and communion with one another.

First, they shall have a full knowledge of one another. There shall be no strangers in heaven. Indeed, it is questioned by some whether the saints shall know one another in heaven, but, truly, there is no question to me, for the saints shall all be of one society; they shall all be of one company; they shall all be of one entire body. And surely it is inconsistent with the glory of that state for one member to have no knowledge of another. If you are of a company here on earth (let the company be 40, 50, 100, or 500) who live together, reside together, converse together, and meet together, you come to have a knowledge of one another. And can it be thought that an eternal abode together in heaven won't give you the knowledge of one another? The Scripture seems very plain and clear in this matter in Matthew 17:1–4: "Jesus taketh Peter, James, and John, and bringeth them up into a high mountain, and there He was transfigured before them." And indeed it was a little corner of heaven that He carried them into there. He brought down Moses and Elijah, and Peter immedi-

ately knew them, and said unto Jesus, "Lord, it is good
for us to be here. If Thou wilt, let us make here three
tabernacles, one for Thee, one for Moses, and one for
Elijah." Peter had never seen Moses and Elijah, for they
had died many years before he was born; yet as soon as
they appeared with Christ, Peter knew them. He knew
which one was Moses and which one was Elijah.

Sirs, the knowledge of the saints won't be decreased,
but rather heightened in heaven. Some of you, it may
be, lie under mourning of spirit for some of your rela-
tives who have gone to heaven. Well, wait just a little
while and you shall know them again. But let me tell
you, you shall not know them after a carnal manner,
but after a spiritual manner. 2 Corinthians 5:16:
"Wherefore henceforth know we no man after the
flesh." Christ shall not be known hereafter after the
flesh, and when you come to heaven you won't know
one another after the flesh; but in a spiritual manner
you shall know one another. Parents shall know their
children, and children shall know their parents in a
spiritual manner. You shall know those servants of God
who have taken pains with you here and helped your
souls on to heaven. Some of you often think, perhaps,
of Reverend Mr. [Thomas] Armitage, who labored with
you in the Lord; and some of you remember Reverend
Mr. [Robert] Allen, who was the Lord's mouthpiece to
you for many years. You who have a hope laid up for you
in heaven shall follow them in your time and in your
order, and shall know them again, and all the servants
of the Lord from one end of the world to the other. You
shall know those whom you have known, and you shall
know those whom you have not known. You shall know
Moses, Abraham, Isaac, Jacob, and all the patriarchs.

Second, you shall know them so as to have communion with them. Matthew 8:11 says that you shall sit down (which is an image of communion) with Abraham, Isaac, and Jacob in the kingdom of heaven. Indeed, all your knowledge of the saints, and all your fellowship with the saints, shall all be resolved into the glorifying of God, so that God shall be uppermost in all. You shall see God through all, and you shall triumph in God and sing praises to God through all, as glorified saints together and as members of the same body. So there will be a fellowship and communion together in the enjoyment of God and in communion with Him.

9. There is a hope which you have laid up for you in heaven of God's being all in all to you. We read in 1 Corinthians 15:28: "And when all things shall be subdued to Him, then shall the Son also Himself be subject to Him that put all things under Him, that God may be all in all." The dispensation that Christ now has in His hand is that He is the Lord of the world; and the government of it shall be laid down when the whole body of believers shall be brought home and all the elect of God's grace brought in. Then shall Christ be glorious in the eyes of the saints, but God shall then be all in all. That is, all believers shall be placed in the immediate presence of God, where shall be the full display of His glory upon them to all eternity, an immediate and powerful display of the glory of the divine majesty upon their souls to eternity.

Here the saints can see the face of God but in a glass (1 Corinthians 13:12). It is but a dim glass that we have here to see God in. But then, says the apostle, it will be "face to face." Moses was importunate when he asked the Lord to see His glory (Exodus 33:18). But the Lord says in verse 20, "Thou canst not see My face, for there shall no man see Me and live." He was saying to Moses, "In your present, mortal state, you are not able to bear My immediate glory. But I will cause some of My goodness to pass before you to satisfy you for the present."

So God makes some manifestations of Himself in the glass of some gospel institutions, but in heaven it will be face to face. We will be in the immediate presence of the Lord, ever to behold His glory. These are some of the blessings that are laid up for the saints in heaven, and which their hopes and expectations should be upon while they are here.

I shall now make a little application of this.

USE 1. If the saints have such a hope laid up for them in heaven, then here you may see the difference between them and the men of this world, who are taken up with the good things that are here below. They cry out, "Who will show us any good?" They look for things that are seen and that are pleasing to the flesh, and they look no further. O sirs! How poorly provided are the men of the world, with all their hundreds and all their thousands, when they have all their good things here and have nothing to come! Do you not see that the portion of God's people is another manner of portion from the portion of the wicked in all their plenty and fullness? The prophet says in Jeremiah 10:16: "The portion of Jacob is not like them." So the portion of a saint is not like the portion of a sinner. Though God has not made you rich in this world, and has not given you the fullness and the honors that the men of this world possess, if you have a hope laid up in heaven for you, has He not dealt better with you? Hagar and her child were sent out of the family with a loaf of bread and a bottle of water, and that was their portion and allowance, while the inheritance was reserved for Isaac (Genesis 21:14). So the Lord gives the good things of this life unto wicked men. He throws these things commonly to them, and they are sent away from His presence with them. And when the loaf is gone and the bottle is empty, they have nothing more to take for themselves. Then they must sit down in eternal misery. Through all the shortcomings that the saints have here, they have a hope that is laid up in heaven. You see, then, that the portion of a saint is not like the portion of a worldly man.

USE 2. See the dignity and the honor that the Lord has put upon all His saints. The worth of a child of God is not known here; like his Lord and Master, he is despised, condemned, and reproached. They are men and women of scorn and contempt, of sorrow and bitterness in the world. But there is honor that the Lord puts upon them, though the world counts them as the offscouring of all things, as those worthies were of whom the world was not worthy. Hebrews 11:36–38: "They had trials of cruel mockings and scourgings; yea, moreover, of bonds and imprisonment. They were stoned; they were sawn asunder; they were tempted; they were slain with the sword; they wandered about in sheepskins and goatskins, being destitute, afflicted, and tormented, men of whom the world was not worthy." And who were these people? They were heirs of heaven, children of the promise. There were persons who had a hope laid up for them in heaven, and in all their disgraces and contempts here they were waiting for a glory that was to be revealed. The Lord has put great honor upon His saints in the hope that is laid up in heaven for them.

USE 3. If there is a hope that the saints have laid up for them in heaven, a hope that will hold, then let all of you look into yourselves and examine your hopes, and see that you are not mistaken in them. There is a hope that will stand you in no stead. We read of the hope of the hypocrite that is like a spider's web; he shall trust in it, and it shall deceive him. O sirs! Look well to your hopes so that you are not mistaken. Consider whether your hope is laid up in heaven, whether you have cast your anchor within the veil. Examine your state and condition to see how it is with you lest, at last, you should miss all this glory that the saints hope for.

And in examining yourselves, look to these two things which the apostle speaks of in the verse before our text: one is faith, and the other is love.

First, look to your faith and see whether you have truly closed with Jesus Christ. True faith unhinges the soul from all things on this side of Christ, and grounds the soul upon Christ Himself. Now if you would know whether your hope is good, see whether your faith is sound. Have you taken the Lord Jesus Christ as yours? Have you taken Him as your Prophet, your Priest, and your King? Have you closed with Him? Have you resigned yourselves up to Him? Examine yourselves about your believing.

Second, examine yourselves about your love. When Jesus Christ put Peter to examining himself, He said, "Simon Peter, lovest thou Me? Simon, lovest thou Me more than these?" His meaning was, "Do you love Me more than all the world, more than your nets, more than all your employments in this world?"

So I ask you, do God and Jesus Christ have the uppermost room in your heart? Are they principal in your affections? Are they more to you than all the world besides? Do you love God and Jesus Christ more than all? Examine yourselves by your faith and by your love, and take heed that you do not take up a false hope that will deceive you.

USE 4. If you have a hope that is laid up in heaven for you, then comfort yourselves with this hope under all the discomforts that you meet with in the world. The apostle makes use of this point in 1 Thessalonians 4:17–18: "Wherefore comfort one another with these words." With what words? "We shall meet the Lord in the air, and so shall be ever with Him." Comfort one another, and comfort your own hearts with these words. You meet with many losses here; you meet with many temptations here; you meet with many afflictions here, trial after trial, one following another. Well, under all these, comfort yourselves with the hope that is laid up for you in heaven. Balance all your trials and temptations with the hope that is in heaven.

USE 5. Last, you who have a hope laid up in heaven for you, see that you walk answerably to your hope. This is expected of you, as the apostle tells you in 1 Thessalonians 2:12: "That ye would walk worthy of God, who hath called you unto His kingdom and glory." See that you walk worthy of the hope that you have received. Have you a hope laid up in heaven for you of such great things as we have mentioned, a hope of ever being with the Lord? Then carry it in a way that corresponds to these hopes, in raised frames, breathings, and longings of heart after God. The hopes of an eternal enjoyment of God in the world to come should fill us with desires after the enjoyment of God here, in those means and according to those ways in which He has promised to let Himself out to His people. You should be continually pressing after the enjoyment of God mediately, you who have the hopes of the eternal enjoyment of God immediately.

Also, the Apostle John says, "He that hath this hope in him purifieth himself, even as He is pure" (1 John 3:3). If you have such a hope, then testify to it by laying siege to corruption, and by seeking to mortify the body of sin and death that you bear around you. Correspond with your hopes in pressing after holiness, and after growth in all grace; for he who has this hope, and he who has the promise of these things, will be perfecting holiness in the fear of God. Make it your business, therefore, to grow in grace and to advance in all holiness, so that you may abound, and that yet more and more in the work of the Lord.

Appendix 2

A Christian's Freedom from Condemnation in Christ

"There is therefore now no condemnation to them
which are in Christ Jesus, who walk not after
the flesh, but after the Spirit." Romans 8:1

This chapter of Romans is, as one has called it, the magazine of a Christian's comfort; it is the cabinet where many jewels are locked up, the ship where much of his treasure is stored. The apostle gives out comfort upon comfort unto believers here.

In the first part of the chapter he endeavors to comfort them under the afflicting and discouraging sense that they had of the remaining corruption that annoyed and pestered them every day, showing that it was pardoned and done away with out of the sight of God.

He endeavors to comfort them under all their trials, tribulations, and afflictions, which were and would be many in this world, and shows them that there was a weight of glory in reserve that would more than balance them all.

He also endeavors to comfort them against their fears of falling away, or of God's casting them off, showing them that nothing shall separate them from the love of Christ. And in the close of the chapter, faith breaks out into a high act, and Paul is able to triumph over all in this world, and over all the principalities of hell and darkness that were engaged against him, showing that in Christ Jesus he was (and all those in his state and condition were) more than a conqueror through Him who loved them.

In the first verse you have a heart-reviving proposition laid down: "There is no condemnation to them that are in Christ Jesus." In the following verses, you have the confirmation of this proposition: "For the law of the spirit of life in Christ Jesus hath made me free from the law of sin and death." In verse 9 he makes application of all unto those in Christ Jesus to whom he had written: "But ye are not in the flesh, but in the Spirit, if so be the Spirit of God dwelleth in you." All you who have the Spirit of God are not in the flesh, but in the Spirit; and therefore there is no condemnation for you. And he proposes it in such general terms that all who have the Spirit may take it up and make application of the comfort thereof to their own souls.

The assertion that he lays down in the text is this: There is no condemnation for those who are in Christ Jesus. This conclusion is drawn from the whole doctrine of our justification in and by the righteousness of Jesus Christ, which he had treated in the preceding chapters of this epistle. Now he concludes from that doctrine that, since we are accepted in Christ's righteousness and are thereby justified before God, there is now no condemnation for us.

So we have in the text the assertion laid down that there is no condemnation to those who are in Christ Jesus. And we have a mark given whereby we may come to know whether we are those to whom there is no condemnation: they are such as do not walk after the flesh, but after the Spirit.

In the proposition or assertion, you may take notice, first, of the subjects, and they are such as are in Christ. You may also take notice of the predicate, and that is that there is no condemnation for them. There are some who make our being in Christ to be our vocation, and they construe our non-condemnation, our justification, and our walking not after the flesh but after the Spirit, to set forth our sanctification. Condemnation is the doom or sentence of a just and righteous judge against an offender. Non-condemnation is the contrary to that, that is, to be acquitted, to be discharged, to have the sentence of death removed and taken off. And this is what God does for all those who are in Christ Jesus. He revokes the sentence that had gone out against them. In the gospel, there is a cancellation of our law-obligation to die. The gospel brings in life and removes the death that the law threatened and pronounced against us. So the proposition from the first part of the verse is this:

DOCTRINE: All those who are in Christ are acquitted, absolved, and discharged by God. "There is now no condemnation to them that are in Christ Jesus." There is no condemnation from God, no condemnation from heaven. God the Father, who is, in Christ, a Father of mercies and a Father of forgivenesses, comes, forgives, and discharges them.

There are three courts, if I may so say: the court of heaven, the court of conscience, and the courts of men. Now a child of God may be sentenced in the two latter ones, and yet be acquitted and cleared in the former one. He may condemn himself, he may draw up charges against himself, and he may write nothing but bitterness against himself while he is acquitted before

God. He may be accused and condemned before men. Jesus Christ was counted a sinner and numbered among transgressors, and yet He was the beloved Son of God all the while. But there is a time coming when all those who are discharged in God's court in heaven shall be cleared, both in the court of conscience and also before the whole world. We shall observe this method in briefly handling the doctrine:

1. Show you the truth of it from Scripture.

2. Give you the properties of this discharge that is given to believers by God.

3. Show you the ground upon which God proceeds in the discharge.

4. Show the time when the soul is taken into this privilege and has the discharge given to him.

5. Make application.

1. Scripture is clear on this: there is no condemnation for those who are in Christ Jesus. They are absolved and discharged by God. Believers are so, but as for all those who are yet in their sins, they are under the sentence of condemnation. It hangs over them and follows them wherever they go. John 3:18: "He that believeth on Him is not condemned, but he that believeth not is condemned already." He is really condemned; he has the sentence really pronounced against him; he is really declared a dead man in the sense of the law. When the judge pronounces the sentence of death against a malefactor, we say that he is a dead man. So everyone who is yet in his sins is a dead man; he is condemned already.

There is indeed this difference between him and one who is in hell: he who is in hell is condemned and executed, but the sinner on earth is condemned and not executed. The sinner in hell is condemned and executed, and there remains no hope for him. The sinner on earth is condemned, and yet there is hope that comes in through the door of the gospel which gives some probability that, if he will stir himself, the sentence may be removed. The patience of God is exercised and drawn out to great lengths, and it is to lead the sinner to repentance. Romans 2:4: "Or despisest thou the riches of His goodness and forbearance and long-suffering, not knowing that the goodness of God leadeth thee to repentance?"

After the sentence, God waits upon the sinner, and will not allow the law to take hold and do its work immediately. The hand of justice is held from smiting, so that the sinner is not presently executed; and in the patience, forbearance, and long-suffering of God a pardon is offered and a way discovered whereby the sinner may come to get free from the doom that is upon him. But the sentence of John 3:36 hangs over the head of every unbeliever: "He that believeth on the Son hath everlasting life, and he that believeth not the Son shall not see life, but the wrath of God abideth on him." The wrath of God hangs over his head in that ancient sentence pronounced against man upon his first transgression. Genesis 2:17: "In the day that thou eatest thereof, thou shalt surely die," or, "thou shalt die the death."

Here is the sentence; here is the doom, and God abides by His Word to this day. Hereupon the apostle says in Galatians 3:10: "For as many as are of the works of the law are under the curse; for it is written, 'Cursed is everyone that continueth not in all things which are written in the book of the law to do them.' " Being under the works of the law, you are under the curse, because the broken law pronounces a curse against all those who break it. So all those who are unbelievers, all those who are under the first covenant, all those who are in a state of sin before God are condemned already.

But all those who are in Christ Jesus have this sentence of death taken off; they are absolved and discharged by the Lord. So says the prophet in Isaiah 38:17: "For Thou hast cast all my sins behind Thy back." God says this after the manner of men. When a man gives back the bond of another, and freely discharges him of the debt, the bond is canceled and is thrown away. It is cast behind his back as wastepaper, nevermore to be made use of, the debt nevermore to be brought into question again, nor yet the debtor brought in on account of the debt. So he says, "Thou hast cast all my sins behind Thy back," that is, "Thou hast given me a discharge so that they shall lie against me no more."

Revelation 2:17: "To him that overcometh will I give to eat of the hidden manna." Manna was a type of Christ. The Apostle Paul makes it clear when he writes to the Corinthians, "He shall eat of the hidden manna," that is, he shall feed on Christ. Every overcomer shall have communion and fellowship with Christ. And that is not all, but "I will give him a white stone." In this expression, the Lord alludes to the custom of the Romans. When a person was tried and found guilty, he was given a black stone as a token of his condemnation, and he who was discharged was given a white stone as a token of his absolution. So Christ says, "I will give him a white stone, and in the stone a new name written, which none knoweth but he that receiveth it." Every overcomer, everyone who is in Christ has a white stone given to him by the Lord. There is no condemnation for those who are in Christ Jesus.

2. I shall proceed to show you the properties of this discharge that the Lord grants to those who are in Christ.

First, it is a real discharge. It is no imaginary thing. It is a real truth that the apostle here affirms. "There is," he says, "therefore now no condemnation to them that are in Christ Jesus." The absolution of a believer is as real as his sinning was, as real as his condemnation was. He was really a sinner, and he was really condemned on account of his sin, and he is just as really discharged. You have the word of the Lord for it. The same Word of truth that tells us there is condemnation to every unbeliever tells us that there is no condemnation for a believer.

But you do not have only the Word of God for it, but you have your discharge under hand and seal. And therefore the apostle tells us that those who believe are sealed by the Spirit of the Lord. The seal of the Spirit is God's seal. Ephesians 1:13: "In whom ye also trusted, after that ye heard the word of truth, the gospel of your salvation, in whom also, after that ye believed, ye were sealed with the Holy Spirit of promise." And Ephesians 4:30: "And grieve not the Holy Spirit of God, whereby you are sealed unto the day of redemption."

The Spirit comes and gives you a sealed pardon. He gives you the seal of God's pardon upon your hearts. And hence the apostle speaks with as much confidence as man can speak upon a sure testimony. 1 John 3:14: "We know that we have passed from death to life." We know it, he says. And "the Spirit itself beareth witness with our spirits that we are the children of God" (Romans 8:16). There is a report and a testimony of the Spirit of God within, and there is, by the work of the Spirit and the hand of the Spirit, the discharge; and the work of God in the discharge is sealed upon the soul of the believer so that he knows as really that he is discharged from his sins as he knew that he was a sinner. A person may be discharged, however, and not know it; for the Spirit of God does not always witness; the Spirit of God does not always seal; nay, He may seal and His seal may be hidden. He may make report and give evidence, and this evidence may be lost. Those who have had the assurance of the pardon of their sins may lose it again. Or it may be some considerable time after the soul has been discharged before he is able to read his discharge; but the Spirit of the Lord first or last will be a witness and sealer to all those who have their discharge, and they shall know it and have the comfort of it. It is a real discharge.

Second, it is a free discharge. God does all that He does for His people *gratis*. There is nothing in His people that has procured and brought in the blessing from the hand of the Lord. But when He comes to discharge a soul, He does it for His own name's sake. Isaiah 43:25: "I, even I, am He that blotteth out thy transgressions for Mine own sake, and will not remember thy sins." God says, "I will blot them out not for your sake, for you have deserved no such thing at My hand. But I will blot them out for My own sake. I do all that I do freely." And therefore Paul says that we are "justified freely by His grace" in Romans 3:24. We are justified freely by the grace of God.

When the sinner deserves the full and effectual execution of the sentence that was pronounced against him, then the Lord comes in a way of free and sovereign grace, and He discharges and pardons. Hosea 14:4: "I will heal their backsliding. I will love them freely; for Mine anger is turned away from them." He will love them freely, He will pardon them freely, He will pass by and forgive them freely. So Colossians 2:13: "And you, being dead, hath He quickened together with Him, having forgiven you all your trespasses." So we read it, but it may be read, "having freely forgiven you all trespasses." God freely forgives the trespasses of His people, those whom He takes unto Himself, those who are in Christ. There we are called upon by the Lord to come to Him without money and without price. "Come, ye that thirst, to the waters; such as have no money, come buy without price. Come and hearken diligently, and your souls shall live" (Isaiah 55:1–3).

Third, it is a full discharge that the Lord grants unto His people, a discharge that takes away all their sins at once. Psalm 103:3: "Who forgiveth all thine iniquities, who healeth all thy diseases." He does not forgive and heal hundreds and thousands of sins only, but all that you are guilty of. All sins of omission, all sins of commission, all sins against the first table of the law, all sins against the second table—they are all forgiven at once. All secret sins, all open sins, all heart sins, all life sins, they are all forgiven.

When a sinner returns to God, he comes with a load of sin upon him; thousands upon thousands of sins he brings with him, and a multitude of sins. And when the Lord receives this guilty soul, He forgives them all at once. Isaiah 55:7: "Let the wicked forsake his ways, and the unrighteous man his thoughts (or, it may be read, the man of wickedness), and let him return unto the Lord, and He will have mercy upon him; and unto our God, for He will abundantly pardon." It may also be read, "He will multiply pardons." Sins have been multiplied in days of ignorance and in days of knowledge, multiplied against all the strivings of the Spirit, multiplied under many tender offerings of Christ, multiplied under many beseechings of the Spirit, multiplied in the clear light of a gospel day. "But," He says, "this shall not keep Me away, for I will abundantly pardon."

God's pardon shall be as extensive as all the sinner's transgressions were. And therefore the apostle says, "There is no condemnation to those who are in Christ Jesus." There is no sin remaining to condemn him of all his repeated transgressions, of all the thousands and ten thousands of sins of which he is guilty. There is no condemnation, not one sin left upon the score to condemn him. Romans 8:33: "Who shall lay anything to the charge of God's elect? It is God that justifieth."

Satan will heap up things against them, but these shall not condemn them. Their own consciences may bring in indictment after indictment against them, but there is nothing that shall stand on record against them, nor anything that shall be laid to their charge to condemn them. None of their sins, be they never so great; none of their sins, be they never so small, shall remain against them. "Who shall lay anything to the charge of God's elect" when God justifies? Therefore the prophet says in Jeremiah 50:20: "The iniquity of Israel shall be sought for, and there shall be none, and the sins of Judah, and they shall not be found for I will pardon them whom I reserve." Their iniquity shall be sought for, and there shall be none found. Why? Because the pardon of God reaches every one of them. Colossians 2:13: "Having forgiven you all trespasses." And Hebrews 8:12: "I will be merciful to their unrighteousness, and their sins and their iniquities I will remember no more."

God is saying, "I will be merciful not to this unrighteousness or to that unrighteousness, but to *all* their unrighteousness—to their sins and to their iniquities." It is spoken of in general terms so that they might know it will reach every particular. It is a full discharge insomuch as the believer is counted righteous; he is constituted as righteous before God. Hebrews 11:4: "By faith Abel offered unto God a more excellent sacrifice than Cain, by which he obtained witness that he was righteous." That is, in his justification in Christ Jesus, in which justification he had absolution, and in the completeness of his justification before God, by God's imputative act, he was reckoned and constituted to be righteous.

Fourth, the discharge that God gives to those who are in Christ is irrevocable. It is such an act of grace that God will abide by and will never recede from, no, not to eternity. Therefore Jeremiah 31:34 says, "I will forgive their iniquities, and I will remember their sins no more." The believer is perhaps afraid that something may be brought in against him at last, that later reckonings may undo his justification. "No," says God, "when I forgive sin, I do it with this resolve of grace, never to remember it again." And therefore we read in Psalm 103:12: "As far as the east is from the west, so far hath He removed our transgressions from us." East and

west can never meet together, so the sins of a believer
that are forgiven by God shall never return again to his
condemnation. The sense of them may return again
and again for his humiliation, but the sins themselves
shall never return again unto condemnation; for God,
having once blotted them out, will never again write
them down. Therefore Romans 11:29: "The gifts and
callings of God are without repentance."

God does all in wisdom, righteousness, and judgment. He knows what He does. He sees all before and
after at the same time. And therefore there can never be
any repentance from God so as to cause Him to recede
from His own act of grace. Having once been absolved,
the sinner shall remain absolved to eternity. Micah
7:19: "Thou wilt cast their iniquities into the depth of
the sea." That which is thrown into the bay may be
washed up again, but take a millstone and carry it out
into the vast ocean, and cast it into the depth of the sea,
and it will never be seen again. And thus the Lord, to il-
lustrate His own grace, makes use of such comparisons
to speak to our understanding. This act of His grace is
done in judgment, and God will never repent of it; it is
an irrevocable act.

OBJECTION. If believers are thus fully and irrevoca-
bly discharged by God, how is it that that God so greatly
afflicts them in the world? How is it that they are seldom free, but are followed with adversity after adversity,
trial after trial, and yet all their sins are done away with?

ANSWER. Though God's people are the people of
affliction and adversity ordinarily in this world, yet
their afflictions are not from wrath, but from love, and
are consistent with His pardoning grace. You must distinguish between punishments that are satisfactory and

punishments that are monitory. You must distinguish between wrath that proceeds from justice and that which proceeds from fatherly corrections and chastisements. God afflicts His people upon two accounts in this world: sometimes for sin and sometimes to try their grace.

God, I grant, sometimes chastises His people for sin. Scripture is clear on that point. Psalm 89:30–33: "If his children forsake My law, and walk not in My judgments; if they break My statutes and keep not My commandments, then will I visit their transgressions with the rod, and their iniquity with stripes. Nevertheless My loving-kindness will I not utterly take from him, nor suffer My faithfulness to fail." Here you see that God chastises for sin. He has reserved to Himself a power to do so. If His children break His law, if they transgress and walk contrary to it, they shall hear of it; they shall feel the smart of His rod. Aye, but it is such a chastisement and visitation as is consistent with the stability of His covenant, for that is not shaken thereby. It is such a chastisement as is consistent with unchangeable love and grace. And by these afflictions God carries on His work in them, the more to humble them and to recover the soul, and to bring it to a due consideration of itself and its ways, in order to obtaining a closer walk with God.

At other times afflictions are for the exercise, trial, and improvement of grace, and all that God might be more glorified. 1 Peter 1:6–7: "Now for a season, if need be, ye are in heaviness through manifold temptations, that the trial of your faith, being much more precious than that of gold that perisheth, may be found unto praise and honor." Afflictions stir up patience, and patience increases experience, and experience increases hope. So under the trial grace is made to abound, and much glory is brought forth to God.

OBJECTION. Aye, the believer is taken near to God and forgiven; but he sins again. Don't his renewed transgressions break his pardon?

ANSWER. Renewed and repeated transgressions are found in those whom God pardons. They may break their peace and take away the comfort of their pardon, but they don't nullify the pardon of God.

Their pardon is continued and renewed as their transgressions are renewed, so that the obligation to punishment, the obligation to hell, and the wrath of God return no more upon their heads. Before God, it returns no more, for the pardon that is given forth by God takes it away; but the sense of the pardon, and all the comforts of the pardon, may be lost for a considerable time. This seems clear from 2 Samuel 12:13: "David said unto Nathan, 'I have sinned against the Lord.' And Nathan said unto David, 'The Lord also hath put away thy sin; thou shalt not die.' " God had blotted out the sin of David, yet if you look at Psalm 51 you will find that the comfort of his pardon was gone; he was not able to read it, nor to derive faith or to take any joy from it. Psalm 51:8: "Make me to hear joy and gladness." That sound seems to be a strange voice in his ears. He was now a stranger to the voice of joy and gladness that he had so often heard from the Lord. "Oh," he says, "if I could only hear that voice again!" And then verse 12: "Restore unto me the joy of Thy salvation, and uphold me with Thy free Spirit." The joy of his pardon was out of sight, and until God returned again to him with fresh consolations, and until the Comforter came to visit him again, he was not able to apply a promise, nor to take in the comfort of his pardon, although the prophet had told him that God had pardoned him. But the obligation to condemnation does not return. As the apostle says in 1 John 2:1: "If any man sins, we have an Advocate with the Father, Jesus Christ the righteous." Christ lies there in heaven to secure the state of a believer, and He keeps up the torrent and stream of God's love to the soul, though the manifestations of that love are under a sovereign rule and disposal.

3. Next I shall give you the ground upon which God proceeds in giving out this discharge to those who are in Christ, and that is the merits and the satisfaction, the propitiation and atonement of Christ Himself. The ground, or the meritorious and procuring cause of all, is the propitiation and satisfaction of Jesus Christ. God the Father pardons, but He must pardon with a respect to His justice. He must pardon in such a way as to secure the glory of all the essential properties of His nature made known to man, either in the first covenant, which was broken, or in the second, in which forgiveness is promised. And that must be a full satisfaction.

Jesus Christ became unto God a Surety for sinners, and He took our sins upon Himself. So, Christ having made satisfaction, God gives a discharge upon that satisfaction. 2 Corinthians 5:21: "For He hath made Him to be sin for us, who knew no sin, that we might be made the righteousness of God in Him." We are made the righteousness of God in Him because the Father has made Him to be sin for us. The Father was pleased to take our sins, lay them upon Christ, and charge them upon Him, and He bore the punishment. 1 Peter 2:24: "Who His own self bore our sins in His own body."

Jesus was herein a sin-offering unto God, like the scapegoat who was but a type of Him. Leviticus 16:21: "Aaron the priest shall come and lay both his hands upon the head of the goat, and confess over him all the iniquities of the children of Israel all their transgressions, and all their sins, putting them upon the head of the goat and then sending it away."

This type belongs to Christ, and the prophet particularly applies it to Him in Isaiah 53:6: "And the Lord hath laid on Him (or, the Lord has made to meet upon Him) the iniquities of us all." He has charged the sin of our nature and the sin of our lives upon Him. He places all our unbelief, all our impatience, all our aberrations, and all our wanderings, both of one kind and of another, all upon Him.

Now hereupon there is a "blotting out of the handwriting of ordinances that was against us" that was contrary to us, and they are all taken out of the way (Colossians 2:14). God the Father comes and blots out all, but it is upon the satisfaction that Jesus Christ gives unto justice. It is done upon the price that the Son of God paid to the Father. Hereupon the apostle says, "Whom God hath set forth to be a propitiation through faith in His blood, to declare His righteousness for the remission of sins that are past" (Romans 3:25). And we are justified freely by His grace, the apostle says. Acts 13:38: "Through this man (that is, the man Jesus) is preached unto you the forgiveness of sins." Ephesians 1:7: "In whom we have redemption through His blood, the forgiveness of sins." Redemption from the law, redemption from the rigor of justice, redemption from all the wrath of God—all this we have through the blood of Jesus. We are, as Ephesians 1:6 tells us, "accepted in the Beloved." We are pardoned, we are constituted righteous, but it is in Christ. Christ Jesus is therefore made righteousness to us. As He was made sin for us, so we are made the righteousness of God in Him. Righteousness from Christ, through Christ, and in Christ is imputed to us. So God does all this upon the merits, the satisfaction, and the atonement of His own Son.

QUESTION. If God pardons sinners in Christ, and discharges them of all their transgressions through His blood, then does God not see sin in His people? If His people sin, are they not sinners before Him?

ANSWER. God does see all the sin that His people are guilty of; they cannot sin unknown to God. He sees every provocation in the heart, and He sees every step that is taken out of the path of His commandments. But the Lord looks upon His people in Christ. As they are considered in themselves, they sin against Him; but now He accepts them in the Beloved. God sees them in Christ, covering all their iniquities and transgressions.

See the likeness to Christ. God the Father saw no sin in Christ, for He was holy, harmless, undefiled, and separate from sinners. There was no sin found in Him. God saw Christ without sin, that is, as He was in Himself. But as He was our Surety, so God laid sin upon Him, and God saw sin that was upon Him. God put Him under obligations to die for our transgressions; and as He was our Surety, so sin was charged upon Him.

Now God the Father sees that we sin daily, as we are in ourselves. But as we are in Christ, we are without sin. So the grace of God in forgiveness is carried on from day to day, notwithstanding our daily failings and imperfections.

4. Next we shall consider when it is that a soul comes to be received into this privilege after he is pardoned and discharged by God. And that is when he comes to believe, and to lay hold of Jesus Christ by faith. I view pardon under a threefold consideration:

First, in the decree of it. It is eternal, for it comes out of the eternal counsels of God.

Second, pardon is to be considered in the purchase of it, and that was in the fullness of time, when Christ was made a sin-offering to God.

Third, pardon is to be considered in the application of it, and that is when a soul is enabled by the almighty power of God to go to Jesus Christ and believe on Him. Acts 13:39: "And by Him all that believe are justified from all things, from which they could not be justified by the law of Moses." When they were under the law of Moses, they could not be justified. The Scripture tells us that there was a time when those who are now discharged were condemned. The Scripture gives abundant testimony of this. Ephesians 2:3: "We were by nature children of wrath, even as others." There is no difference naturally between you who are pardoned and those who have gone to hell. There is no difference in your childhood, no difference in your grown age.

In 1 Corinthians 6:9–11, the apostle speaks of great sinners, and such, he says, shall not inherit the kingdom of God. "And such were some of you, but now ye are washed, but now ye are justified." You were under the sentence of condemnation as well as others, but now you are washed, now you are pardoned, now that you believe. Therefore, the righteousness by which we are justified is called "the righteousness of faith" in Romans 9:30: "What shall we say then? That the

Gentiles, which followed not after righteousness, have attained to righteousness, even the righteousness which is of faith." It is the righteousness of faith because it is apprehended by faith on the soul's part. It takes hold of it by faith. Romans 5:1: "Being justified by faith we have peace with God."

So until the soul comes to believe, to have this faith to rely on the Lord Jesus Christ for righteousness, he is not justified. Galatians 3:22: "The Scripture hath concluded all under sin, that the promise by faith of Jesus Christ might be given to them that believe." All are concluded to be under sin, all are under the sentence of condemnation; every child born into the world is concluded to be under sin and under the sentence of condemnation by reason of sin. But the promise of salvation is by faith on Jesus Christ; the promise of salvation and forgiveness, the promise of righteousness and peace, is given unto "them that believe."

So when the sinner is translated, when he is brought over to Christ, when he has faith wrought in him to believe in the Lord Jesus Christ, then he is pardoned. And following the loss of your pardon (I mean, the sense of the loss of it), upon the renewal of faith and the stirring up of fresh acts of faith, the sense of pardon returns, and consolation and joy return.

USE 1. If God thus discharges sinners in Christ, then this truth calls upon all of you to study this discharge of the gospel more fully so that you may understand this wonderful proceeding of gospel grace. Sirs, this point is a fundamental point; it is one of the foundational truths and principles of the gospel—and therefore, whatever you neglect, do not neglect the study of this mystery.

There are other truths of great concern. There is no truth, no principle of the gospel but is worth your inquiring into. But this is one of the main ones, and if you are off here, you are off in all. The more you know of this one, and the more savingly you understand this privilege, the more you will be led into other privileges, and the higher your consolation will be. This is even a Benjamin, as I may so call it. When Joseph came to serve his brethren, as we read in Genesis 43:34, "He sent messes to them from before him, and Benjamin's mess was five times as much as any of the others." Truly, the importance and value of this truth are such that you need to study this point five times more than some others. The apostle says in 1 John 4:9, "In this was the love of God manifested," to provide a propitiation and atonement, to provide a blood through which forgiveness of sins should be dispensed. In this is the love of God manifested, and you should study this truth so that you may understand something of the height, depth, length, and breadth of the love of God manifested unto you herein. Dive into this mystery.

USE 2. Labor to clear up your own discharge unto your own soul. Many are the doubts and fears that believers labor under, and they arise from darkness in this point. Could they but have faith that there is no condemnation for them, their fears would vanish, their doubts would be answered, and their souls would be filled with the joy of God their salvation.

Now there are some ways whereby this may be made clear:

1. There is the witness of the Spirit of God. This is a satisfying testimony to all who have it. It puts all out of doubt and answers a thousand questions at once. Once

the testimony of the Spirit comes within, all fears vanish; all mists and clouds that affected the understanding flee away and are scattered.

2. It is evidenced by a lively faith in the promise of forgiveness; from thence the soul is enabled to take in the comfort of the discharge.

3. Sometimes our justification is made clear to us from our sanctification. But truly, that satisfaction that comes to a soul through his searches into the work of sanctification in the soul is but small. It is coming and going, because the work of grace upon our hearts is under so much weakness, and is oftentimes cloudy and dark, so that a believer, many times, can hardly tell whether he has any grace in his heart or not. But that satisfaction which comes in by the help of the Spirit of God through the actings of faith upon the promise of forgiveness, and that which comes in through the immediate testimony of the Spirit of God in our hearts— this is far more refreshing and satisfying to the soul. Labor after the assurance of this discharge, so that you may know that you have a part in the promise of forgiveness.

USE 3. You who are forgiven, you whom the Lord has thus discharged, ought to walk thankfully and live in the admiration of that grace that is glorified in this act of God towards you. Psalm 116:12–13: "What shall I render to the Lord for all His benefits?" That is what we should say for all our common mercies, though never so small. "What shall I render to the Lord? I will take up the cup of salvation and call upon the name of the Lord." And if this is what we should say for ordinary mercies, what shall we say to the Lord for great ones?

You have been brought up in a land of vision, perhaps under a religious education, and have sat under a powerful gospel ministry, where you have been told of your sins, invited and called to return to God, and exhorted to believe on the Lord Jesus Christ, Yet, it may be, you went on in a way of sinning against God for 10, 20, 30 years before God laid hold of you. And after such a long course of rebellion, and after you had run out in all manner of extravagance, or at least in your heart did commit all manner of iniquity, and had it in your heart to do a great deal more than the preventing grace of God would allow you—after all this disobedience and rebellion, in a moment, as it were, God came and pardoned all.

The prodigal son, a great rebel, was yet received and embraced in his father's arms, and not one word of objection was made against him. He was received as if he had never gone out of his father's house or grieved him. What wonderful grace is this! Sirs, it is stupendous grace for God to make His approach to a poor soul, to press forgiveness upon it, to blot out your transgressions as if with a thick cloud. Isaiah 44:22: "I have blotted out, as a thick cloud, thy transgressions." The Lord has blotted out, like a thick cloud, your transgressions, and has caused the sun of His love to break through and scatter all at once.

You should admire the greatness of God's grace, that so many treasons should be forgiven at once, and that so many years of transgression against God should be forgiven at once. I remember how the sufferings of Jesus Christ are spoken of in Scripture. When He saw what a cup of wrath there was in His Father's hand, it is said that He was amazed and astonished when He saw all the wrath that was to be poured out upon Him! And if even Jesus Christ was amazed when He saw all the wrath that was to be poured out upon Him, do you see all the grace that the gospel has brought forth for you? Do you see all this grace, and does it not amaze you that God should do so much for such a sinner as you are, for one so unworthy, so undeserving, so provoking as you are?

I remember how taken Abigail was taken with the kindness and condescension of David, when he sent to her to take her. 1 Samuel 25:41: "She arose and bowed herself on her face to the earth and said, 'Behold, let thine handmaid be a servant to wash the feet of the servants of my lord.' " It is as if she was saying, "What! Does King David, the Lord's anointed, send for me? It is more than I deserve should he only make me a handmaid to wash the feet of his servants!" She was amazed at his love and condescension. And, sirs, does not all the grace of God that is laid out on you, in freeing you from hell and in blotting out all your transgressions, so that they shall never be remembered against you—does not all this grace amaze you?

I remember a passage of Solomon's in 1 Kings 8:27, when God afforded His presence in the temple. Solomon said, "Will God indeed dwell on the earth? Behold, the heaven and the heaven of heavens cannot contain Him; how much less the house that I have built!" Will God indeed dwell on the earth? Oh, Solomon was taken with the condescension of grace, that God should stoop so low as to fill with His glory that house which Solomon had built for Him!

Oh, sirs, has God filled your hearts with His glory, with the glory of His pardoning love and grace? Oh, then, say, "What! Lord, wilt Thou dwell with me? What!

Lord, dost Thou pass by all my rebellion and all my backsliding, and wilt Thou receive me into Thy love and favor?" Oh, then, magnify, admire, and live in the admiration of this grace that God has thus wrought for you!

USE 4. Has the Lord pardoned and discharged your souls, so that there is now no condemnation for you? Then think with yourselves what returns of love you ought to make unto this God who has done so much for you. If you were taken captive by the Turks and were cruelly used in their bondage, and if a friend should hear of your misery and captivity, and should come and pay the price of redemption, set you free, and bring you back to your own country, you would never forget the love of this man if you had any gratefulness in you. All the love that you could manifest to him you would always think too little, and it would come far short of his love for you.

But, sirs, what is the love of such a friend in such a case when compared to the love of God in your soul's case! He has taken away the sentence of condemnation that was against you when you were ready to die. He saved you from wrath and hell, and assured you that none of your sins would ever rise up to your condemnation. Nothing shall ever be laid to your charge, because God has discharged you; all that you can do for this God is to love Him, and you will manifest ingratitude indeed if you do not stir up your love for this God. Psalm 31:23: "O love the Lord, all ye His saints."

"Aye," you say, "they have reason to do it. They are saved from hell, delivered from going down to the pit! They have thousands and thousands of transgressions forgiven at once!" Oh, it becomes those who are thus dealt with to love God. Sirs, you should love Him with a heart-love; you should love the Lord with all your hearts and with all your souls. Here the whole strength of your affections should go out. You should love God with a transcendent love; you should love Him above all; you should love Him with an abounding love.

It is said in Luke 7:47 that Mary loved much. She had many sins forgiven, and much love, abounding love followed. The higher your sins were, the greater is your pardon, and the greater your love should be. You should love God with a love of complacency, so as to joy in Him and take up your delight in Him.

God loves you with such a love. He is said to rest in His love towards us. Zephaniah 3:17: "The Lord thy God in the midst of thee is mighty. He will save thee, He will rejoice over thee with joy. He will rest in His love." Now, shall God take complacency in such a poor, vile creature as you are, and do so much in the greatness of His love for you, and will you not take your delight in God? You should love God with an abiding love; you should dwell in your love for God; you should live in your love for God. Jude 21: "Keep yourselves in the love of God." Your love to God is something you should love and cherish at all times, so that you will always live in love for God. You should do all that you do in love for God; love Him with an abiding love.

USE 5. You whom the Lord has discharged, be always ready to discharge and forgive others wherein they provoke and offend you. As the apostle says concerning love in 1 John 4:11: "Beloved, if God so loved us, we ought also to love one another." So I may say in this case that, if God has forgiven us, we ought also to forgive one another.

Solomon tells us (and truly I think it is a Scripture that a great many do not understand in practice) in Proverbs 19:11 that "it is the glory of a man to pass over a transgression." Many do not think so; they think that it is the nobleness of their spirits to stand and argue out a point, to have satisfaction upon such an injury or upon such and such provocation. He is counted of a poor, pusillanimous spirit who passes over such things, who bears affronts and makes nothing of them. But, says Solomon, it is his glory. It is the crown of a man to pass over a transgression because, the more you forgive others, the more you manifest the sense of the grace of God in forgiving you. We are taught by Christ to pray, "Forgive us our debts, as we also forgive everyone who is indebted to us." Can you say in your heart, when you go to God for forgiveness, that you have freely forgiven your brother, your sister, or your neighbor who has offended you, who has wronged and injured you? Luke 17:3–4: "Take heed to yourselves; if thy brother trespass against thee, rebuke him; and if he repent, forgive him. And if he trespass against thee seven times in a day, and seven times in a day turn again to thee saying, 'I repent,' thou shalt forgive him.' "

In Matthew 18:23–35 the Lord gives us a parable of a servant: "The Lord had compassion on him, and forgave him the debt; and the same servant went out to his fellow servant that owed him a hundred pence, and he took him by the throat, saying, 'Pay me that thou owest me.' " Here is set forth the spirit of the children of men: they would have forgiveness from others, but they will not forgive others. Well, but when Peter came to Christ and said, "Lord, how often shall my brother sin against me and I forgive him? Till seven times?" Jesus said to him, "I say not unto thee until seven times, but until seventy times seven." As often as he offends, so often you shall forgive.

USE 6. This doctrine calls for an abhorrence of all papal masses as propitiatory sacrifices for sin. You who have heard anything of the grace of God in the forgiveness of the new covenant, do you detest and defy the idolatry and the abominations of the church of Rome, that would pretend to forgive sins? What is this but to wrong the grace of God? What is this but to trample upon the blood of the covenant as an insufficient thing? No, pardon of sin does not come at so cheap a rate as to be bought with money; but it comes in at the door of free grace, through the blood of Jesus. Thousands of rams, ten thousand rivers of oil, and the first-born of the body for the sin of the soul, these will not satisfy; for they and their money will perish together who would buy pardon of sin at such a price. Bless God that you know better, and let it raise up in you an abhorrence of that religion that would thus corrupt you.

QUESTION. Ah, but how shall I come to get God's discharge sealed upon my soul? Oh, if I had the evidence and witness of this, all would be well.

ANSWER 1. Come before God with confessions in your mouth. Bewail and spread your transgressions before Him. Psalm 32:5: "I acknowledged my sin unto Thee, and my iniquity have I not hid. I said, 'I will confess my transgressions unto the Lord,' and Thou forgavest the iniquity of my sin." David confessed; he came and judged himself before God; he came and lamented his sinful condition and his sin-guiltiness before God. He lamented and bewailed, he poured out his confessions before God, and the Lord came and visited his soul with pardon, with the sense of forgiveness.

ANSWER 2. Plead with God for His pardon and urge His promise for forgiveness. This is what the servants of the Lord have done when they have lacked the sense of pardon. Psalm 51:1: "Have mercy upon me, O God, according to Thy loving-kindess; according to the multitude of Thy tender mercies blot out my transgressions." When sin lay against Israel, and God began to threaten, Moses stepped up and pleaded with God for pardon. So the servants of the Lord have all along pleaded with God for pardon when they lacked it. Do this, and urge God with His promise of forgiveness.

ANSWER 3. Have your eyes upon Jesus Christ. Pardon comes through His blood; it is merited, it is purchased by Jesus Christ. Look unto Him, and put forth renewed acts of faith upon Him. In renewing your closing with Him, and in resigning yourself by faith to Him, you may come to have your pardon sealed.

ANSWER 4. Wait upon God in sealing ordinances. It may be that you have wronged your soul to this day, that you have walked at so great a distance from God in His sealing ordinances. If you had gone and attended upon God, it may be that you would have had some hint of His pardoning love for you that would have more fully satisfied your soul. I remember what God said to Gideon, promising that if he would go and listen, he would hear something that would strengthen him (Judges 7:10–11). So I say, wait upon God in those ordinances where God gives out strengthening grace, and where God seals up His love for His people, and there you may find something that will be a feast to your soul. There you may meet with something that may confirm this love of God toward your soul, and put out all doubt for you more than ever.

As for you who have the sense of God's discharging love in your hearts, I have three things to leave with you:

First, improve the sense of God's love unto an influence to all duties, and to all obedience to God. Let the sense of His kindness to you be so improved and wrought upon your hearts as may constrain you to devote and dedicate yourselves to God in your whole course, and to lay yourselves out in all duties of obedience to God more than ever. And know that you can never serve this God enough; you can never do enough for this God who has done so much for you. Labor to do more for Him than ever, to serve Him with a better heart and with a better spirit, to pray often and with greater fervency, to confess with more sincerity, and to walk with God in more exactness. Lay yourselves out to the utmost in this work.

Second, extend your pity and compassion to those who are yet in a condemned state. Your souls should mourn over those who are yet in their sins. You know what it is to be under sin, and you know what it is to be under grace; therefore, your hearts should be full of compassion for those who are yet in that state which, by grace, you are delivered from. Ebed-melech's compassion and tenderness to the prophet is recorded in Jeremiah 38:11: "He took men with him, and went into the house of the king under the treasury, and took with him old cast clouts and old rotten rags, and let them down with cords into the dungeon." O sirs! Your compassion should go out to those who are yet in their sins! I remember what David promised God in Psalm

51:12–13: "Restore to me the joy of Thy salvation, and uphold me with Thy free Spirit. Then shall I teach transgressors Thy ways, and sinners shall be converted unto Thee." He would then make it his business to turn sinners to God; he would make it his business to convince and awaken, and draw others out of their sinful state, that is, to labor with them if by any means the Spirit of God may work upon them. Be full of compassion toward others who are in a state of condemnation.

Third, and last, keep up and walk in a humble sense of your great transgressions that God has forgiven you. Sirs, though God has forgiven your sins, yet you should remember them. You should remember them so as to walk humbly and softly before God all your days, that you did ever provoke so gracious a God by such heinous provocations and enormities.